# HISTORICAL ANTHOLOGY OF MUSIC

Baroque, Rococo, and Pre-Classical Music

# Historical Anthology

## OF

# *MUSIC*

### BY

## ARCHIBALD T. DAVISON AND WILLI APEL

BAROQUE, ROCOCO, AND PRE-CLASSICAL MUSIC

39810

# HARVARD UNIVERSITY PRESS
## *CAMBRIDGE, MASSACHUSETTS*

LIBRARY OF CONGRESS CATALOG CARD NUMBER 49-4539

ISBN 0-674-39301-5

PRINTED IN THE UNITED STATES OF AMERICA

# PREFACE

THE first volume of the *Historical Anthology of Music*—Oriental, Medieval, and Renaissance Music—contained material illustrating the history of music from antiquity to the end of the sixteenth century. The present and final volume continues the *Anthology* to about 1780. The only composers of first rank whose music has been omitted from the collection are Bach and Handel; their works are universally available, and the editors have preferred to select characteristic works of important composers whose music does not come so readily to hand.

Choosing the material has been more difficult than was the case with the previous volume. The period closing with 1600 produced mainly works of relatively small dimension; but the years which this new volume covers abound in large-scale compositions such as operas, oratorios, concertos, and cantatas. So while it is possible to select a single madrigal which embodies a good many of the features of Thomas Morley's writing, the problem of choosing one, two, or even three examples of the varied style of Monteverdi or Gluck cost the editors a deal of thought. They cannot pretend to have dealt inclusively with the music of an era in which drastic changes of style took place within the lifetime of a single composer. Long consideration was accorded every piece, and although opinion is bound to differ regarding the wisdom which dictated the final choice, the editors hope that, in the main, the contents of this volume will be held to be reasonably characteristic of the period it represents.

The problem of selection was not the only taxing issue which confronted the editors. In a work such as this compromises are an obvious necessity. No single air from an opera, for example, may form the basis of a proper stylistic study if removed from the musical context in the scene to which it belongs; no one section of an anthem or motet may be fully understood unless its particular significance in the entire composition is recognized. Although not all the shorter forms cast in sections are subject to this consideration, it would appear, nonetheless, that as the art advances the integration of one movement of a work with all the other movements becomes more and more a matter of importance; and in the period dealt with in this volume it cannot be ignored. Yet compromises must be made if the size of the volume is to be kept within bounds. In some cases, therefore, although the editors realized that it would be ideal to include all the sections of an anthem, let us say, limitations of space forced them to do otherwise.

Another necessary type of compromise must be adopted when a composer makes certain slight changes in the repetition of a musical section. It would be ideal, of course, to reproduce exactly the repeated section with, say, its three or four very minor rhythmic changes; but to do so would add little to one's knowledge of the music and would needlessly increase the size of the volume. It has been the editors' purpose, however, that no salient discrepancy between the source and the present version shall be ignored, and to this end these discrepancies are accounted for in the Commentary. Still another space-saving method is invoked when the vocal bass and the figured bass frequently coincide. In this case a single staff has been used for both, the notes of the vocal bass being indicated by upward stemming, the continuo by downward stemming, and where the same note belongs to both by double stemming.

As in the earlier volume, repetitions of passages of text with which, by the time they are encountered, the reader is presumably familiar, have been omitted; they are indicated by a few dots after the first word or two of the passage. Again as in the first volume, the translations are for the greater part literal, and aim as far as is feasible to follow the word-by-word progress of the original. Only in the case of passages drawn from the Scriptures have literary questions been given weight.

The realizations of the thorough-bass aim at a spontaneous and quasi-improvisatory keyboard style rather than a pseudo-contrapuntal style based on observations of the rules of strict counterpoint. Realizations have been omitted where they would merely be a duplication of the vocal or instrumental parts. In a few elementary cases no realization has been offered in order to afford the student an opportunity for practice. With the exception of Numbers 224, 269, and 271, which are the work of Mr. Erwin Bodky of Cambridge, all the credit for the arduous and important labor of realizing the figured basses should go to Dr. Apel.

In the preparation of the musical material the earliest obtainable source for each selection has been consulted. Where modern editions were available they, too, have been cited in the Commentary as being of practical aid to the student. A list of phonograph records as complete as the available sources will allow has also been included in the Commentary. As far as the editors are aware there has been selected no recording which provides an unauthentic or misleading performance, such as that of a harpsichord piece played on a piano-forte.

Progress on a plan mentioned in the preface to the first volume may be reported here: negotiations toward the recording of a part at least of the contents of both volumes of the *Anthology* have been undertaken.

During the progress of the work connected with the assembling of this volume some changes in the original plan had to be made. As a result of these changes certain references which occur in the *Harvard Dictionary of Music* will be found to be inaccurate. Any confusion, however, may be immediately resolved by reference to the index to the present volume.

As supplementary reading the editors recommend Manfred F. Bukofzer, *Music in the Baroque Era* (New York: W. W. Norton, 1947), and Donald J. Grout, *A Short History of Opera* (New York: Columbia University Press, 1947); references to both these books will be found in the Commentary.

The editors gratefully acknowledge their indebtedness to the following, who generously made available certain selections: Professor M. F. Bukofzer, of the University of California, for No. 308; Dr. Henry Clarke, of the University of California at Los Angeles, for No. 243 and the note in the Commentary which accompanies it; Mme Suzanne Clercx-Lejeune, of Brussels, for No. 298; Professor Alfred Einstein, of Smith College, for Nos. 186, 203, 220, and 302 (reproduced with the kind permission of the Music Department of Smith College); Dr. Hugo Leichtentritt, of Cambridge, for No. 267; Professor Henry Mishkin, of Amherst College, for Nos. 219, 259, and 263; and Mr. John M. Oldenburg, of New York, for No. 271.

Also to Father Alex. J. Denomy, C.S.B., of the Pontifical Institute of Mediaeval Studies in Toronto; Professor Urban T. Holmes, Jr., of the University of North Carolina; and to Professor George B. Weston, of Cambridge, goes our appreciation for many of the translations.

Sincere thanks are due as well to Miss Jean Macleod, of Pittsfield, for the preparation of a number of scores for the copyist, and to Mr. Elmer Olsson, Mr. Leonard Holvik, and Mr. W. C. Cummings, Jr., of Cambridge, for their reading of the music manuscript. Mr. Cummings, in particular, gave most generously of his time in making a final check of the material. This long and painstaking labor both merits and receives the heartfelt gratitude of the editors.

An earnest effort has been made to present a volume as free from errors as is humanly possible. The editors hope that readers will make known to them anything that stands in need of correction.

For the editors,
A. T. D.

April 3, 1950

# CONTENTS

*(Numbers refer to item rather than to page)*

## CHAPTER I

### EARLY BAROQUE MUSIC
——— (1600–1640) ———

## CHAPTER II

### MIDDLE BAROQUE MUSIC
——— (1640–1680) ———

# CHAPTER III

## LATE BAROQUE MUSIC
——— (1680–1750) ———

# CHAPTER IV

## ROCOCO AND PRE-CLASSICAL MUSIC
——— (1730–1780) ———

## COMMENTARY AND TRANSLATIONS

BAROQUE, ROCOCO, AND PRE-CLASSICAL MUSIC

# I. Early Baroque Music (1600-1640)

## 182. Jacopo Peri (1561-1633)

Funeste piaggi

Recitative from *Euridice*

I

degl'oc- chi mie- i Mi- sero Mi- sero e in su quell'o- ra Che scaldar-mi à bei rag- gi io

mi cre-de- i Mor- te spen-se il bel lu- me e freddo e so- lo restai fra il pian-to e il duo- lo Co-

me an- gue suol in fredda piaggia il ver- no La-cri-ma-te al mio pianto Om- bre d'in-fer- no.

## 183. Emilio de' Cavalieri (1550?-1602)

A questi suoni

*From Rappresentazione di anima e di corpo*

CORPO

A questi suo-ni e can- ti Al- ma mo-ver mi sen- to Co- me la foglia al ven- to.

ANIMA

Co- me ti cangi pre- sto? Stà for- te, e non te-me- re: Questo è fal- so piace- re.

PIACERE E COMPAGNI

1. O canti, ò ri-si, ò gra- ti-o-si a-mo- ri, Fresch'acque, prati molli, au-re se-re-

2. sti leggiadre, e di- let-to-si oi-do- ri, Tri- on-fi e fe-ste d'al- le-grezza pie-

ne: Grate armo-nie, che ral-le-grate i co-ri; Con-vi-ti, pasti e sa-po-ri-te ce-ne; Con-

ne, Di-let-to, gusto giu-bi-lo e pia-ce-re, Be-a-ta l'al-ma, che vi può go-de-re.

vi-ti, pasti e sa-po-ri-te ce-ne.

RITORNELLO

REPEAT FROM 𝄋
TO ⊕;
THEN SKIP
TO ⊕

82. Ve-

⊕ [ANIMA]

Non vi cred'io, nò nò, Li vostr'in-ganni io sò; Tut-te le vo-stre co-se, Che pai-on di-let-

to-se Al fin son tutte a-ma-re; Be-a-ta l'al-ma che ne sà man-ca-re.

## 184. Giulio Caccini (1550?-1618)

Sfogava con le stelle

Aria

Sfo-ga-va con le stel-le Un infer-no d'a-more Sotto nottur-no cielo il suo do-lo-re, E dice a fisso in

lo-ro O o imma-gini bel-le d'el i-dol mio ch'a-do-ro, Sì come a me mostra-te Mentre così splen-de-te La sua

3

ra- ra bel- ta- te Cosi mostraste a le- i, Mentre cotanto ar- de- te I vi- vi ardo-

ri mie- i La fa-re-ste co'l vostr'au-reo sem- biante, Pie-to-sa sì, pie- to-sa sì co-

me me fa- te a-man- te, la fa-re-ste col vostr'au-reo sem-biante Pie-to-sa sì, pie-to- sa sì come me fa-

te a- man-te, co- me me fa-

Trillo

te a- man- te.

### 185. Lodovico Grossi Viadana (1564-1627)

Exaudi me, Domine

Concerto Ecclesiastico

Ex- au- di me Do- mi- ne, ex- au- di me Do- mine, quo-niam be- nig-na est

Basso per sonar nell'organo

4

quo-ni- am be- nig-na est mi-se-ri-cor-di- a tu-      a      mise- ri- cor- di-a tu-

a: Se- cundum multi-tu-di-nem mi-      se-ra-ti- o-num tu- a-rum re-      spi-ce      in me

re- spi-ce      in me.      Et ne a- vertas fa-ci-em tu-      am a pu-e- ro tu-o

a pu-e- ro tu-o      a pu-e- ro tu-      o:  Quo-ni-am tri-      bu- lor tri-

bu-lor, ve-lo-                          ci-ter ex-au-di me ve-lo-

ci- ter ve- lo-ci-ter ex-au- di me ve-lo- ci- ter ex- au- di me.

## 186. Adriano Banchieri (1567?-1634)

Il zapaione musicale

Madrigal Comedy

## 187. Claudio Monteverdi (1567-1643)

Ma che temi

Recitative from *Orfeo*

ma chi me'l nie-g'ohi-mè sogn'o vaneggio Qual occul-to poter di questi or-ro-ri da questi a-mati or-

ro ri mal mio gra-do mi tragge e mi con-du-ce a l'o-di-o-sa lu-ce.

## 188. Claudio Monteverdi

Ohimè, se tanto amate

Madrigal

9

# 189. Claudio Monteverdi

Non schivar, non parar

From *Il combattimento di Tancredi e Clorinda*

ne scen- de ta- glio_in van ne punta_a vo- to

l'onta irrita lo sdegno alla vendetta alla ven-det-ta e la vendetta poi e la vendetta poi l'onta ri-no-va

On- de sempre_al ferir sempre_al ferir sempre alla fretta stimol novo s'aggiunge e-pia-ga nova

piano

d'hor in hor più si me-sce e più ri-stret-ta si fa la pu-gna e spa-da oprar non giova; dansi con po-mi e in-fe-lo-ni-ti

Qui si lascia l'arco e si strappano le corde con duoi diti

forte

e crudi Coz-zan con gli el-mi in-sie- me e con gli scu- di.

# 190. Vater unser im Himmelreich
## Four Chorale Preludes

a. Samuel Scheidt (1587-1654)

## b. Dietrich Buxtehude (1637-1707)

## c. Johann Pachelbel (1653-1706)

d. Johann Sebastian Bach (1685-1750)

Canzona francese

For Harpsichord or Organ

## 192. Girolamo Frescobaldi (1583-1643)

Partite sopra l'aria della Romanesca

Keyboard Variations

18

## 193. Girolamo Frescobaldi

Toccata IX

For Organ

NON SENZA FATIGA SI GIUNGE AL FINE

## 194. Girolamo Frescobaldi

Canzona

For Harpsichord or Organ

## 195. Heinrich Scheidemann (1596?-1663)

a. Praeludium

Organ Prelude

b. Praeludium

Organ Prelude and Fugue

## 196. Samuel Scheidt (1587-1654)

Wehe, Windgen, wehe

Keyboard Variations

1. VARIATIO

2. VARIATIO

12. Variatio

Imitatio Violistica

26

## 197. Johann Hermann Schein (1586-1630)

Intrada

For Ensemble

## 198. Giovanni Battista Fontana (d. 1630)

Sonata

For Violin and Continuo

Orig. ¢ 3 o. d o

[Adagio]

[Allegro Moderato]

## 199. Biagio Marini (1600-*c*.1660)

Romanesca

Variations for Violin and Continuo

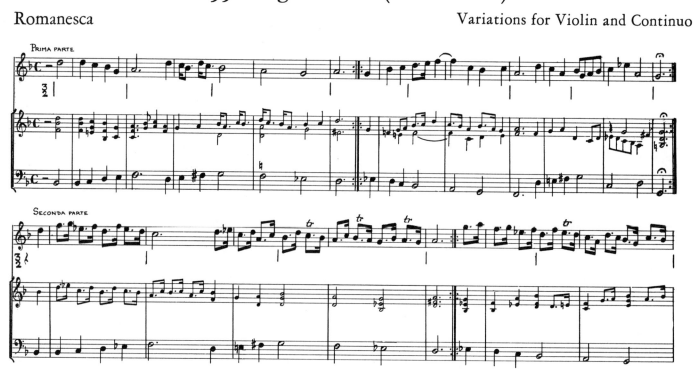

## 200. Manuel Rodrigues Coelho (c.1580-1623?)

Verso do primeiro tom

Verset for Voice and Organ

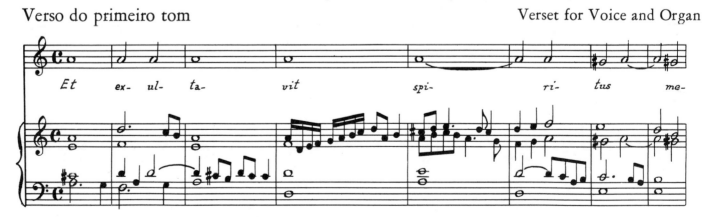

Et ex- ul- ta- vit spi- ri- tus me-

us ... in ... De- o sa-lu-
ta- ri me- o.

# II. Middle Baroque Music (1640-1680)

## 201. Heinrich Schütz (1585-1672)

a. Da Jesus an dem Kreuze stund

Chorus from *Die sieben Worte*

## b. Und um die neunte Stunde

35

# 202. Heinrich Schütz

Saul, was verfolgst du mich

For Double Chorus and Instruments

39

# 203. Luigi Rossi (1598-1653)

Chamber Cantata

Io lo vedo

Io lo ve-do, ò lu-ci bel-le, Ch'il mio ar-dire è più ch'ar- di-re; Ma non pos-so non se-

gui-re La mia stella e le mie stel-le. Ma non pos-so non se-gui-re La mia

stella e le mie stel-le. Il pen-sier quand' è ch'io gi-ri A voi, ca-ri lu-mi a-

ma-ti, Sul mio lab-bro, non chia-ma-ti, Se ne ven-go no i sos- pi-ri, Ne fre-

nar pos-so i de-si-ri Che mai sem-pre al cor mi stan-no Ò per for-za ò per in-gan-no

Con di- lu- vio di fiam- mel- le.  Io lo

## 204. Henry Lawes (1596-1662)

Sweet Echo

Air from *Masque of Comus*

Sweet Echo, sweetest Nymph, that liv'st un-seen within thy ai- ry shell by slow Meander's margent green And in the vi- o-

let embroidered vale where the lovelorn Nightingale nightly to thee her sad song mourneth well, Can'st thou not tell me

of a gentle Pair that lik- est thy Narcissus are  O if thou have hid' them in some flowry cave  tell me but

where, sweet Queen of Parley, Daugh- ter of the Sphere. So maist thou be trans- plan-ted to the Skys

And hold a Counterpoint to all Heav'ns Har- mo- nies.

## 205. Heinrich Albert (1604-1651)

Auf, mein Geist

Aria

Auf, mein Geist! Und nun er he- be Gottes Güt' und Va- ter- treu,

Er ist, der so lang ich le- be Mich macht al- ler Sor- gen frei. Drum auch Ihm al- lein zu

Eh- ren Sich mein Spiel soll lassen hö- ren.

Symphonia

Two more
stanzas.

## 206. Francesco Cavalli (1602?-1676)

Ecco la lettra

Recitative and Aria from *Xerxes*

Arsamene [Aria]

me, voglio ser-vir vi af-fè.

In-na-mo-ra-to cor trà- fit- to del do- lor di

per- fi-da bel-tà, la morte a- vanza, al-tra vi- ta non hà che la spe- ran-

za. La morte a- vanza, al-tra vi- ta non hà che la spe- ran- za.

Arsamene:

Va ch'in ogni momento il cor t'el

Elviro: Si-gnor, m'era scor-da-to voi mi di-ceste nò non va fe-li-ce.

di- ce.

Va fe-li-ce.

Eh dite-me-lo no?

O, o così la-sciate far a me.

Arsamene:
Repeats Aria with
new text.

44

# 207. Giacomo Carissimi (c.1604-1674)

**Miserunt ergo sortem**

Recitative and Chorus from *Jonas*

orum, accensus est furor tuus et contra me tem-pe- stas or-ta est et infremue- runt

venti et fluctus intumu-e- -runt vallavit me a-byssus et cetus, et cetus de-glu-tivit me. Num quid in e-ternum proje-

(Violins)

cisti servum tu-um? Placare, Domine, ignosce, Domine, et mise-re- re, et mise-re- re.

## 208. Steffano Landi (c.1590-c.1653)

Sinfonia

From *Il San Alessio*, Act II

 Vls.1, 2,3

Arpe, Liuti, Tiorbe e Violoni

Basso e Continuo per Gravicembali

49

## 209. Steffano Landi

Poca voglia di far bene

Duet from *Il San Alessio*

# 210. Tarquinio Merula (fl. 1615-1652)

Canzon detta la Vesconta

For Instruments

## 211. Denis Gaultier (c.1605-1672)

Mode sous-ionien

For Lute

## 212. Jacques Champion de Chambonnières (c.1597-1672)

Chaconne

For Harpsichord

## 213. Andreas Hammerschmidt (1611-1675)

Wende Dich, Herr

Dialogue

55

# 214. Franz Tunder (1614-1667)

Wachet auf, ruft uns die Stimme·

Chorale Aria

macht euch be- reit, macht euch be- reit zu der Hoch- zeit, zu der Hoch- zeit,

[Adagio]

ihr müsset ihm ent- ge- gen, ent- ge- gen gehn.

## 215. Franz Tunder

Praeludium

Prelude and Fugue for Organ

Ped.

Ped.

## 216. Johann Jakob Froberger (1616-1667)

Lamento

For Harpsichord

# 217. Johann Jakob Froberger

Toccata II

## 218. Johann Rosenmüller (*c.*1619-1684)

Aleph. Ego vir

From *Lamentationes Jeremiae*

A- leph. E- go vir vi-dens paupertatem meam in virga indignati-o-nis

in virga indignati-o- nis e- ius. A- leph. Me minavit, et adduxit in tenebras, et

non et non in lu- cem. A- leph, A- leph. Tan-tum in me vertit, et con-

vertit manum suam to- ta di- e. *Beth.* *Vetustam fecit pellem meam, et carnem meam, con-*

tri- vit ossa me- a. *Beth.* *Aedifica-vit in gyro me-o, et circum-dedit me*

fel-le et la- bo- re. *Beth.* *In tene-bro-sis col-lo-ca-vit me,*

ut non e-gre-di- ar; ag-gra-va-vit com- pe-dem me- um. *Ghi-* *mel. Sed et cum cla-*

ma-ve-ro et ro-ga-ve-ro, ex-clusit orati-onem me-am. *Ghi-* *mel. Conclusit vias meas la-pi-dibus*

ADAGIO ALLEGRO

quadris, semitas me-as sub-ver- tit. *Je-ru-sa-lem, Je-ru-sa-lem, Je-ru-sa-lem, Je-ru- sa- lem convertere, con-*

vertere, convertere ad Do-minum, convertere, con-vertere, convertere ad Do- minum, ad Do-                 mi-                 num,

Do-          minum De-                                                                    um tu-    um.

## 219. Maurizio Cazzati (c.1620-1677)

Sonata prima La Pellicana                    For Violin and Continuo

LARGO E VIVACE

PRESTISSIMO

# 220. Giovanni Legrenzi (1626?-1690)

**La Buscha**

Sonata for Instruments

72

73

## 221. Marc' Antonio Cesti (1623-1669)

Di bellezza e di valore

From *Il pomo d'oro*

## 222. Francesco Provenzale (*c.*1630-1704)

Lasciatemi morir

From *Il schiavo di sua moglie*

*Largo*

Menalippa

Lascia-te mi, las-

Orchestra

cia- te mi mo-rir stel- le cru- de- li! Ch'il vi- ver tra ne- mi- ci

e schia-vi-tù, ch'il vi- ver tra ne- mi- ci e schia-vitù Se la cadu-ta mi- a la su ne

cie-li fu sta-bi- li-ta, non risorgo più, non risorgo più.

Se la ca-du-ta mi- a la su ne cieli fu sta-bi- li-ta non ri-sor- go

78

più, non ri-sor-            go più.

L'ar-      mi      non so-no mai      non sono mai      d'a-mor fe- de-      li. Las-

cia- te mi,  las- cia- te mi mo-rir,  stelle cru-  de-li, stel-  le crude- li, las-cia-te mi morir,  stel-

le cru-de-      li.

# 223. Robert Cambert (1628?-1677)

Overture

From *Pomone*

## 224. Jean-Baptiste Lully (1633?-1687)

Overture

From *Alceste*

Gai

### 225. Jean-Baptiste Lully

Le Ciel protège les héros

*Eole*

Le ciel pro- tè- ge les Hé- ros: Al- lez, Ad- mète, allez, Al-

ci- de, Le Dieu qui sur les eaux pré- si- de M'ordonne de cal- mer les flots: Al- lez, al- lez, pour-sui-vez un per- fi- de. Retirez

vous, retirez vous. Vents en cour- roux, Rentrez dans vos prisons pro- fondes, rentrez dans vos prisons pro- fon- des Et lais-

sez ré- gner sur les on-

des, les Zé- phirs, les Zé- phirs les plus doux, Et lais- sez, et lais-

sez ré-gner sur les on-                                                                                                    des,

les Zé-phirs, les Zé-phirs les plus doux, les Zé-phirs, les Zé-phirs les plus doux.

## 226. Marc Antoine Charpentier (1634-1704)

Dialogue entre Madeleine et Jésus

Magdalena

Hei, hei mi-hi in-fe-lix Mag-da-le-na! hei, hei mi-hi in-fe-lix in-fe-lix Mag-da-

le-      na, tu-le-runt Do-minum me-um, quem a-mabam, qui di-li-ge-bat me, in quo vi-ve-bam, qui pro

me mo-ri di-gna-tus est. Et ne-sci-o, u-bi po-su-e-runt e- um. Hei, hei mi-hi in-felix Magda-

le- na! hei, hei mi-hi in- fe-lix in-fe-lix Mag-da-le- na!

**Magdalena**

Do- mi- ne, si me sus-tu-lis-ti Christum

**Jesus**

Mu- li- er, quid plo-ras? quid sus-pi- ras? quem que-ris?

me- um, di- ci- te mi-hi, u- bi po-su-is-ti e- um, et e-go e-um tol- lam! Ma-

Je- su mi!

ri- a! No- li me tan-ge- re, no- li! non-dum e- nim as-cen-di ad Pa-trem

meum, Va- de au- tem ad fra- tres me- os et dic e- is: "As- cen- do ad Pa- trem

me- um, as- cen- do ad Pa- trem me- um et De- um ves-

trum; De- um me- um et De- um ves- trum." Li- ce-

at mi- hi, Do- mi- ne, stig- ma- ta sa- cra tan- ge- re.

No- li me tan- ge- re.

No- li os- cu- la- ri pla- gas tu- as?

No- li me tan- ge- re, no- li.

88

# 227. Joan Cererols (d. 1676)

Señor mio Jesu Cristo

Villancico

# 228. Adam Krieger (1634-1666)

Adonis Tod

Aria with Ritornellos

Wo muss der schöne Jä- ger sein, A- do- nis mei-ne See- le? umb den ich in ver- lieb-ter Pein mich of-te plag' und quä- le.

Ritornello I. Adagio.
[Vls]
[Vlas]

O bittre Pein, über die wohl nichts kann sein: ein wil- des Schwein hat den er- schla-gen, Ach! ach! ach!

ach! den ich e- wig muss be- kla- gen. O Angst und Not! O Angst und Not! Ach A- do- nis ist

tot! O Angst und Not! Ach A- donis ist tot! Mein Ado- nis ist tot! Ach Ado- nis ist tot! O Angst und Not! Mein Adonis ist

92

*Ritornello II. Adagio.*

tot! O Angst und Not!

## 229. Louis Couperin (1630-1665)

Menuet de Poitou

For Harpsichord

DOUBLE PAR Mᴿ COUPERIN

# 230. Matthew Locke (*c.*1632-1677)

Fantazia

## 231. Nicolas Antoine Le Bègue (1630-1702)

Noël, "Une vierge pucelle"

For Organ

## 232. Jean Henri d'Anglebert (c.1628-1691)

Prélude, Allemande, Sarabande

From a Suite for Harpsichord

PRÉLUDE

ALLEMANDE

Sarabande. Lentement

## 233. Esajas Reusner (1636-1679)

Prelude

For Lute

## 234. Dietrich Buxtehude (1637-1707)

Praeludium cum fuga

Organ Toccata

## 235. Dietrich Buxtehude

Liebster Herr Jesu

1. Vers

Soprano I

Lieb-ster Herr Jesu, wo bleibst du so lange, so lange, so lan-ge, so lan-ge, wo bleibst du, wo bleibst du so lan-

ge? Komm doch, mir wird hier auf Er-den sehr ban- ge, mir wird hier auf Erden sehr

ban- ge. Komm doch und nimm mich, wenn dir es ge-fällt, Komm doch, komm doch und nimm mich wenn dir es ge-

fällt, von der be- schwerlichen Bür-de der Welt. Liebster Herr Je-su, wo bange.

Da capo al 𝄋 e poi: Fine

Vl. Fl. 1

Vl. Fl. 2

## 2. Vers

Es ist ge-nug, Herr, drum komm zu er- lösen mei-ne be- drän-ge-te See- le vom Bö-sen, ich bin von Kla- gen und

Seuf-zen so matt, und der verdriesslichen Trä-nen so satt, so satt, so satt, und der verdriesslichen Trä-nen so satt.

Komm nur, Herr Je- su, Komm, Komm, komm nur, Herr Je- su, wo bleibst du so lan- ge? Komm doch, mir wird hier auf

Komm nur, Herr Je-su, komm, komm,

Er- den sehr ban-ge, sehr ban- ge, sehr ban- ge, sehr ban-ge, Komm doch, mir wird hier auf Er-den sehr ban- ge.

sehr ban- ge, sehr ban-ge, Komm...

sehr ban- ge, sehr ban- ge,

## 236. Alessandro Poglietti (d. 1683)

Aria allemagna con alcuni variazioni

For Harpsichord

PARTE 15ᵃ FRANZÖSISCHE BAISELEMANS

PARTE 17ᵃ POLNISCHER SABLSCHERTZ

## 237. Johann Christoph Bach (1642-1703)

Praeludium und fuge ex dis

For Organ

# 238. Heinrich Franz Biber (1644-1704)

Surrexit Christus hodie

Variations for Violin and Continuo

## 239. Juan Cabanilles (1644-1712)

Paseos

For Organ

## 240. Georg Muffat (c.1645-1704)

Passacaglia

# 241. Alessandro Stradella (1645?-1682)

Tra cruci funeste

Più presto che si può

Trà cru-ci fu- ne- sti all' em-pio s'ap- presti di morte cru-

de-le di morte cru-dele acer-bo ri- gor

a-cerbo ri- gor. Gelo-so fu- ror nell'alma_in-fie-

rita à torre di vita l'iniquo in-fe-dele, l'iniquo in-fe-dele gli spirti m'af-fret-      ta.

Vendetta, ven-det- ta, ven-det-ta, ven-det-      ta, ven-det-

ta, vendetta, ven-det-      ta, vendetta, ven- det- ta.

*Ritornello*

# 242. Pelham Humphrey (1647-1674)

O Lord, my God

Verse Anthem

## 243. John Blow (1648-1708)

Mourn for thy servant

Chorus from *Venus and Adonis*

## 244. Agostino Steffani (1653-1728)

Un balen

Aria from *Henrico Leone*

## 245. Giovanni Battista Vitali (c.1644-1692)

Sonata La Graziani

For Two Violins and Continuo

*Vivace*

# III. Late Baroque Music (1680-1750)

## 246. Giuseppe Torelli (1650?-1708)

Opus VIII, No. 8
Last movement

Solo Concerto
For Violin and Orchestra

127

## 247. Johann Kaspar Ferdinand Fischer (*c.1660–c.1738*)

Prelude and Fugue                                        For Organ or Harpsichord

## 248. Johann Kaspar Ferdinand Fischer

Suite

For Harpsichord

## 249. Johann Krieger (1649-1725)

a. Ricercar

For Organ

b. Fuga

## 250. Johann Pachelbel (1653-1706)

Suite ex gis

## 251. Johann Pachelbel

Magnificat Fuga

For Organ

# 252. Arcangelo Corelli (1653-1713)

**Opus V, No. 3**
First and second movements

Sonata da chiesa
For Violin and Orchestra

# 253. Arcangelo Corelli

Sonata da camera
For Violin

## 254. Philipp Heinrich Erlebach (1657-1714)

Himmel, du weisst meine Plagen

Aria with Ritornello

Him-  mel, du weisst mei-ne Pla-

gen,   dir, nur dir   sind sie be- kannt.

# 255. Henry Purcell (1659-1695)

Thy hand, Belinda

From *Dido and Aeneas*

144

## 256. Henry Purcell

Fantasia

For Viols

# 257. André Campra (1660-1744)

Cantate Domino

Motet for Two Solo Voices

Sopran 2

Exultabunt sancti, Exultabunt sancti in glo - ri-a, Excul - ta-bunt san-cti in glo - ri-a,

laeta- buntur, laeta-buntur in cu-bi-libus su - is. Excul- tabunt san-cti in glo - ri-a, in

glo- ri-a, Exultabunt sancti in gloria, in glo- ri-a: laeta- buntur, laetabuntur in cu-bi-libus su-is.

Sopr. 1. Exal-ta-ti-o-nes De-i in gutture e-o- rum: et gladi-i ancipites in manibus e-o- rum.

Sopr. 2. Ad faciendam vindictam in natio- ni-

Sopr. 1. Ad al-li-gan -

dos reges e-orum in compe-dibus,

bus: increpa-ti-o-nes in po-pu-lis.

Sopr. 2. Ad al-li-

149

# 258. Alessandro Scarlatti (1659-1725)

Mitilde, mio tesor

*Recitativo*

Mitilde, Mitilde, mio te- sor, così ve- lo- ce dunque da me t'invola il rio destino; ahi, che a' cader vi-

cino e'il fior de miei con- tenti nel duol d'a- spri tormen- ti. Tu solingo mi lasci qui dove vi aspre balze alti di-

rupi miro ombrosa campagna, che spirando ter- ror spavento e morte mi- naccia al viver mio l'ul- ti-ma sorte.

*Aria. Larghetto*

Tu ben sai l'amare stille che ver-sai da questi lumi, cara speme ca-ra, ca-ra, cara

spe-me del mio cor. Tu ben sai, tu ben sai l'amare stille che versai da questi lu - mi, cara speme, cara,

152

cara, cara speme del mio speme, cara, cara, cara speme del mio cor.                    E mi-

ra-sti le scintille ch'avvam-pando il petto mi-o mi fer vitti- ma, vit-ti-ma d'a-mor.          E mi-ra-sti le scintil-le ch'avvam-

[fine]

pan-do il petto mi-o mi fer vit-tima, vit-ti-ma d'a-mor, mi fer vit-          ti-ma d'amor.     Ma con chi par-lo,   oh

Recitativo

Da capo al fine

Dio, chi ascolta i miei la-menti, ah, ch'all'aure spie-tate,  ai sordi venti, ai tronchi, ai sassi, all' insensate piante in

Aria. Allegro moderato.

van, in van favel-la questo labre amante.                    Selve ombro-

153

se, Selve ombro- se, piante anno- se, voi tempra-

te, temprate il mio pe- nar, il mio pe- nar. Selve om- bro-se, piante an-

no-se, voi tem-pra- te, voi temprate il mio pe- nar, voi tempra- te, voi tem- pra-

te il mio pe- nar, il mi- o pe- nar. Così al- meno il mio seno tre-

[fine]

gua al du- ol potrà spe- rar, po- trà sperar. Così al-meno il mio seno tre- gua al duol potrà spe-rar, potrà, potrà spe-

rar    tre-gua al duol,    po-trà sperar, potrà, potrà sperar.

*Da capo al fine.*

## 259.  Alessandro Scarlatti

Sinfonia avanti l'opera

From *La Griselda*

# 260. Alessandro Scarlatti

**Concerto No. 3**

First three movements

Largo

**Allegro**

161

## 261. Johann Kuhnau (1660-1722)

Der todtkranke und wieder gesunde Hiskias

Program Sonata for Harpsichord

*Il lamento di Hiskia per la morte annonciatagli e le sue preghiere ardenti.*

*La di lui confidenza in Iddio.*

L'allegrezza del Rè convalescente.

si ricorda del male passato

se ne dimentica

adagio

allegro

adagio

allegro

164

## 262. Giovanni Battista Bononcini (c.1672-c.1752)

Deh lascia, o core

Aria from *Astianatte*

Deh lascia o core di re-spi-rar per un mo-men- to, Deh lascia o co- re di sospi-rar per un mo- men- to. Deh lascia o co- re di so- spi-rar, deh lascia o co- re di sospi-rar per un mo- men- to, deh lascia o cor di sospi-rar per un mo- men- to.

E tor- na e torna poi con più do-

ler A la-cri-mar chio mi con-ten- to, E tor-na poi con più do- ler A lacrimar chio mi contento, chio mi con-

ten- to, con più do- ler A la-cri-mar chio mi con-ten- to, chio mi con-ten-

to. Deh lascia o

Dal segno al Fine.

## 263. Tommaso Antonio Vitali (c.1665-c.1747)

Sonata No. 4

Trio Sonata
For Violins and Continuo

Grave

Vlc.+Org.

## 264. John Christopher Pepusch (1667-1752)

**a. My love is all madness**

From *The Beggar's Opera*

My love is all madness and fol-ly, a-lone I lye, toss tum-ble and cry, What a hap-py creature is Pol-ly, Was e'er such a wretch as I. With rage I red-den like scar-let That my dear in-con-stant varlet Stark blind to my charms Is lost in the arms Of that jilt, that in-veig-ling harlot! Stark blind to my charms Is lost in the arms Of that jilt, that in-veig-ling har-lot! This, this my re-sent-ment a- larms.

**b. Hither, dear husband**

From *The Beggar's Opera*

Polly: Hither, dear hus-band, turn your eyes    Think with that look, thy Pol-ly dies

Lucy: Be- stow one glance to cheer me

## 265. Francois Couperin (1668-1733)

a. Le Rossignol en amour

For Harpsichord

*Double de Rossignol.*

*legato*

## b. Sœur Monique

For Harpsichord

*Tendrement, sans lenteur.*

Rondeau

1er Couplet

Rondeau
to §

## 266. François Couperin

Qui dat nivem

Motet for Solo Voice

174

## 267. Reinhard Keiser (1674-1739)

Fahret wohl

Duet from *Adonis*

176

## 268. William Croft (1678-1727)

Put me not to rebuke

Anthem

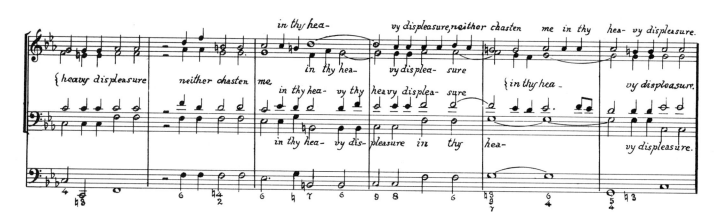

## 269. Evaristo Felice dall' Abaco (1675-1742)

Opus III, No. 2
Second movement

Trio Sonata
For Violins

# 270. Antonio Vivaldi (1680?-1743)

Opus III, No. 6
First movement

Concerto Grosso
For Strings and Continuo

Allegro

Violone e Cembalo

186

# 271. Georg Philipp Telemann (1681-1767)

Sonata  
First movement

For Flute, Violin, Violoncello,  
and Harpsichord

## 272. Georg Philipp Telemann

Chor der Seligen

From *Tag des Gerichts*

un- ser Gott, der Her- re Ze- ba- oth.

## 273. Francesco Durante (1684-1755)

Fiero acerbo

Duet

Fie- ro acerbo destin dell'alma mi-a pe- no lan-guis- co e
Fie- ro a- cerbo de- stin dell'al ma mi-a pe- no lan-guisco

mo- ro e mo- ro, pe- no lan-guisco e mo- ro e mo-
e mo- ro e mo- ro, pe- no lan-guis- co e mo- ro e mo-

# 274. Domenico Scarlatti (1683-1757)

Sonata

For Harpsichord

## 275.  Giuseppe Tartini (1692-1770)

Opus III, No. 12
Last movement

Sonata
For Violin and Continuo

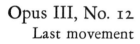

## 276. Jean Philippe Rameau (1683-1764)

Ramage des oiseaux

From *Le Temple de la Gloire*

200

vers.       Ces   oi-   seaux   par   leur   doux    ra-

ma-     ge   Em- bel- lis-     sent   nos      certs;

Ils    an- non- cent dans leur lan-      ga-        ge     Le   bon-

heur    de   l'u- ni-  vers,    Le   bon- heur

de         l'u-  ni-   vers.

Ré-pon- dez    à  leur  chant,   voix er-  rante   et fi-  dè-  le:          E-

très doux

doux

fort en adoucissant

cho, frap- pez les airs des sons har-mo-ni- eux.

fort en adoucissant

(V<sup>elles</sup>, C.B. et Clavecin)

Repetez a- vec moi: ma gloire est im- mor- tel- te, Je

rè-                                                                      gne

(Clav. et un pupitre de V<sup>elle</sup>)

sur un peu- ple heu- reux.

Ces oi- seaux par leur doux ra- ma-

## 277. Jean Philippe Rameau

"Sommeil," Rondeau tendre

From *Dardanus*

# 278. Jean Marie Leclair (1697-1764)

Opus V, No. 12

First movement

Sonata
For Violin and Continuo

Adagio

## 279. Maurice Greene (1696?-1755)

**Acquaint thyself with God**

Anthem

be --- ac-quaint thy self and be at peace with God    and lay up his words

lay up his words in thine heart    acquaint thy self with God and lay up his words in thine heart, lay up ---

lay up ---    lay up his words in thine heart.

**Andante vivace**

If thou re-turn to the Al-mighty    put away in-

i-quity put away in-i-quity from thee put away ---    If thou re-turn to the Al-

mighty          to ---                    put away in-i-quity in-i-quity from thee      put away ---                              put a-way in-

i-quity     from     thee    put away ---

## 280. Theophil (Gottlieb) Muffat (1690-1770)

Final

From a Suite for Harpsichord

*Final. Allegro.*

# IV. Rococo and Pre-Classical Music (1730-1780)

## 281. Johann Adolf Hasse (1699-1783)

Ma giunge appunto

Recitative from *La conversione di Sant' Agostino*

si- sti- lo ed in lui rino- va il co- re, ricon- du- ci- lo al fi- ne, al tuo so- a-

ve a- mo- re. Agostino: 8 A- mi- co, ah, quai tor- men- ti quai tormen- ti

sof- fre il mi- sero co- re! Ah, santa fe- de, ti co- no- sco, t'a- do- ro! Ma, oh Di- o, che mi co-

man- di? La- sciar dovrò per sempre i vie- ta- ti ma dol- ci af- fet- ti del mio co- re? Ah, se po-

Alipio:

tes- si... 8 A- mi- co, tutto puoi, se Dio t'as- siste; e in pugna co- sì gra- ve E- gli t'assiste- rà.

213

## 282. Karl Heinrich Graun (1701-1759)

Godi l'amabile

Cavatina from *Montezuma*

l'im-pre-sa se- guita a cui t'in- vi- ta un dol-ce e tene-ro, un dol-ce e te- nero, so-a-

ve a- mor, so- a- ve a- mor.

Fls.
Vls.

Vla.

Vlc., etc.

Gedi l'a- ma- bi-le presente i-

Fls.

Vls.+Vla.

stan- te ch'e il ve-ro ed u- nico ben della vi- ta; dal ti- mor li- be-ra, ama il tuo a- mante, l'im-pre-sa

se- guita a cui t'in- vi-ta un dol- ce e te- nero, un dol-ce e te- nero, so-a- ve a- mor, so-a-

mor,    l'im-pre-sa    se-guita    à    cui    t'in-vi-ta    un    dol-

ce    e    te-nero,    so-a-    ve a-    mor,    so-a-    ve a-    mor.

## 283. Giovanni Battista Sammartini (1701-1775)

Symphony in D-major

First movement

For Orchestra

[ALLEGRO]

# 284. Giovanni Platti (*c.*1700-after 1740)

Opus I, No. 2
Fourth movement

Sonata
For Harpsichord

## 285. Baldassare Galuppi (1706-1785)

Da me non speri

From *Il filosofo di campagna*

Da me non speri d'a-ver un soldo se il ma- ni- gol- do ve-des-si

li. Se se n'è an-da-ta, se si è spo-sa-ta, da me non ven-ga, non ver-rò qui. Chi ha a- vu-to, ha a-vu-to,

Chi ha fatto, ha fat-to; chi ha a-vu-to, ha a-vu-to, chi ha fat- to, ha fat- to; non son si mat- to, non vuo' get-

gi- ta da me co- si    non vuo'do-ta- re    la figlia ar-di- ta    che se n'è gi- ta da me co-si,    non vuo'do-

ta-re    la figlia ardi-ta    che se n'è gi- ta da me co-si,    da me co- si,    da me co- si.

## 286. Giovanni Battista Pergolesi (1710-1736)

Le virtuose

From *Il maestro di musica*

Le vir-tu- o- se    che son fa-mo-    se    che son fa-mo-

se in fa,    mi,    re,    in fa, mi    re    son tutte sta-te sot- to di me,    tutte tutte

223

tut- te sot- to di me. Le no- te fer- me, le ful- mi-

na- te, tril- li, ca- den-

ze, ar- ci- sal- ta- te,

tut- to tutto an po- tu- to da me impa- rar, tut- to da me tut- to tutto an po-

tu- to da me im- pa- rar.

Le vir- tu- o- se che son fa- mo- se, che son fa- mo- se in
fa, mi, re, in fa, mi, re son tut- te sta- te sot- to di
me, tutte tutte tut- te sot- to di me. Le no- te fer-
me, le ful- mi- na- te,
tril- li, ca- den-

ze, ar- ci- sal- ta-

te, tut- to tut- to an po- tu- to da me im- pa- rar. Le no- te

fer- me, le ful- mi- na- te, tril- li, ca- den- ze ar- ci- sal- ta- te, tut- to tutto an po- tu- to da me impa-

rar, tut- to tut- to da me impa- rar.

# 287. Giovanni Battista Pergolesi

Lo conosco

Duet from *La serva padrona*

la-te, gli occhi ed io voi di-con no, no, no, ed è un so-gno questo qui, sì,

sì, sì, sì, ed è un so-gno que-sto qui.

Mà per-chè? Mà per-chè? Non son i-o bella,

gra-zi-o-sa, e spi-ri-to-sa? Su mi-ra-te: leg-gia-dri-a, leg-gia-dri-a, ve'che bri-o, che

bri-o, che ma-e-stà, che ma-e-stà!

(Ah, co-stei mi va ten-tan-do

(Ei mi par che va ca-lando, va ca-lando.) Sì, si- gno- re.

quan-to va che me la fa, che me la fa.) Eh, van-ne

Ri- sol- ve- te. Son per voi gli af-fet-ti mie-i, e do- vre-te spo-sar

vi- a. Eh, mat-ta se- i.

me, do- vrete, do- vrete, do- vrete spo- sar me, spo- sar me.

Oh ch'im- broglio, ch'im-broglio, ch'imbroglio egl' è per me, egl' è per me.

Lo co- nosco sì a que- gli occhiet-ti fur- bi, la-dri, ma- lignet-ti.

Signo-

mie-i, e dovre-te sì,  sì,  sì, sì,  sì, sì,  do- vrete, do-vrete, do-

siete,  signo-ri-na, no,  no,  no,  no,  (Oh, che im-broglio, ch'imbroglio, ch'im-

vrete spo- sar me,  spo-sar me.

broglio  egli è per me,  egli è per me.)

*unis.*

## 288. Wilhelm Friedemann Bach (1710-1784)

Polonaise II

For Harpsichord or Pianoforte

## 289. Wilhelm Friedemann Bach

Fugue IV

For Harpsichord or Pianoforte

## 290. Thomas Augustine Arne (1710-1778)

Come, O come my dearest

From *The Fall of Phaeton*

O come, o come my dearest, and

233

hi- ther bring thy lips a-dorn'd with all the blooming spring, thy lips a-dorn'd with all the bloom- ing spring.

A thousand, thousand sweets their fragrant a- toms blend which in a gale of joy, which in a gale of joy thy

breath at-tend: Thy love in gentle murmurs to my soul ap-ply, Heal me with kisses, Oh! heal me with

kis-ses or else I die or else I die.

End with the first symphony.

# 291. Jean Jacques Rousseau (1712-1778)

Allons danser

From *Le Devin du village*

Allons dan-ser sous les or- meaux, animez vous jeu-nes fil- le- tes, allons dan-ser sous les or- meaux, Galans pre- nés vos cha- lu-meaux.

Répetons mil- le chan-so-net-tes, et pour a- voir le coeur joy-eux Dan- sons a-vec nos a- moureux, mais n'y res-tons jamais seu- let-tes: allons dan-ser

À la ville on fait bien plus defra-cas, mais sont ils aussi gai dans leurs é-bats,

Toujours con-tens, toujours chan-tans, Plaisir sans art, Beauté sans fard, Tous leurs con-certs valent ils nos mu-set-tes? allons dan-

# 292. Christoph Willibald Gluck (1714-1787)

Chiamo il mio ben

From *Orfeo*

## 293. Christoph Willibald Gluck

Diane impitoyable

# 294. Johann Stamitz (1717-1757)

Opus V, No. 2
First movement

Symphony
For Orchestra

Presto

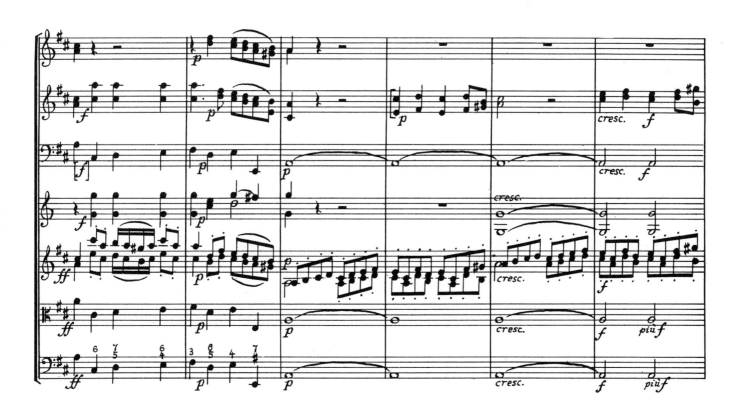

# 295. Georg Matthias Monn (1717-1750)

Symphony in D-major

For Orchestra

Last movement

*Allegro*

## 296. Karl Philipp Emanuel Bach (1714-1788)

Fantasia

For Pianoforte or Clavichord

# 297. Karl Philipp Emanuel Bach

Sonata
Second movement

For Pianoforte
or Clavichord

*Cantabile*

## 298. Domenico Terradellas (1713-1751)

In vasto mare infido

Motet for Solo Voice

250

cu - ra    tu Stel-la Cy- no- su-ra    tu nos de- fen-

(segue)

de  tu Stella Cy-  no- su-ra  tu nos de-fen-

(segue)

(segue)

de  tu  nos de- fen-    de.                                                    In

I+II

f

f            f

va- sto mare in- fi- do    in   no- cte tam obscu- ra    tu  Stel- la Cy- no-su-ra    tu

p

p

Stel- la Cy- no-su- ra    tu  nos de-fen-

de tu  nos de-fen-

de  tu Stel- la  tu  nos de-fen- de    tu nos de-fen-    de  tu  nos de-fen-

I+II

II

de de-fen-    de.

I+II

f

f

Fin.

Coe-

252

les- tis au- ro- ra no- ctis fu- gan- do hor- ro- res no- ctis fu- gan- do hor- ro- res et

vo- ces et cla- mo- res be- ni- gna at- ten-

de be- ni- gna at- ten- de at- ten- de.

I+II

Da Capo dal 𝄋

253

# 299. Niccolò Jommelli (1714-1774)

Mors et vita

Motet for Solo Voices

## 300. Nicola Piccinni (1728-1800)

Achetez à ma boutique

From *Le Faux Lord*

ti-que,   choisis- sez    à vostre goût,    choisissez à vostre goût.

Je con- ten- te ma pra-ti- que,    a-che- tez, je tiens de tout,    je con- ten- te ma pratique, ache-

tez,   a- che- tez,    je tiens de tout, je tiens de tous, je tiens de tout.

Irene: Qu'entends je?

Ga-ze de Bo- lo-gne, bonne eau de Co- lo-gne, veste de Ly- on,  beau point d'Alen- çon,  acier d'Angle-ter-re, bas fins de Beau-

cai-re, rubans de Pa- ris, aiguil-les tres belles,  epingles, den- tel-les,    tout à ju- ste prix,

unis.   Vla

257

tout à ju-ste prix. Ache- tez, a-che- tez. Gaze de Bo- lo-gne, bonne eau de Co- lo- gne, veste de Ly-

on, beau point d'Alen- çon, a- cier d'Angle- ter- re, bas fins de Beau- cai- re, ru-bans de Pa- ris, aiguil-les tres

bel-les, epingles, den- tel-les, tout à ju- ste prix, tout à ju-ste prix. Ache-tez, ache-

tez, ache- tez.

## 301. Johann Adam Hiller (1728-1804)

Bald die Blonde, bald die Braune

From *Lisuart und Dariolette*

Allegretto

Derwin:

Bald die Blonde, bald die Braune, bald die Magre, bald die Dicke: o die wunder-li-che Laune, o der schöne Schmetter-ling! Bald die Blonde, bald die Braune, bald die Magre, bald die Dicke: o die wunder-li-che Laune, o der schöne Schmetter-ling! o die wunder-li-che Laune, o der schöne Schmetter-ling! Ei- ner einzgen sanften Blicke sich mit Seel und Leib verschreiben, lass ich gel- ten; doch potz Vel- ten! Im- mer hin und her zu treiben, im- mer hin und her zu treiben, ist ein

gar zu ar-ges Ding, ist ein gar zu ar-ges Ding; im-mer hin und her zu treiben, im- mer hin und her zu treiben, ist ein

gar zu ar-ges Ding, ist ein gar zu ar-ges Ding.

## 302. Giovanni Maria Placido Rutini (c.1730-1797)

Opus VI, No. 6
Last movement

Sonata
For Harpsichord or Pianoforte

261

# 303. Johann Christian Bach (1735-1782)

**Opus XVII, No. 4**
First movement

Sonata
For Pianoforte

# 304. Johann Friedrich Edelmann (1749-1794)

**Opus I, No. 1**
First movement

Sonata
For Violin and Pianoforte

266

# 305. Karl Ditters von Dittersdorf (1739-1799)

Schlaflied des Sturmwald

From *Doctor und Apotheker*

(schläft und schnarcht)

ha! ha! komm' an.

perdendosi

# 306. André Ernest Modeste Grétry (1741-1813)

Et zic et zic

From *Richard Cœur-de-Lion*

Un peu plus vite

[Refrain]

Et zic et zic et zic et zoc, Et fric et fric et

Petite Flûte[al'ottava con Vl.1]

Vl.1

Vl.2

Vla. f

Vlc., Contrebas, Basson

268

Chorus (Paysannes et Paysans)   §   Couplets

froc, Quand les boeufs vont deux à deux, Le la- bourage en va mieux. Quand les boeufs vont deux à deux, Le labourage en va mieux. 1. Sans ber-
2. Qu'en di-
[men an octave below]

ger, si la ber-gè- re Est en un lieu so- li-tai-re, Tout pour elle est en-nuy-eux; Mais si le ber-ger Syl- vandre Au-près
te vous, ma com-mère? Et qu'en pen-sez vous, mon com-pè-re? Rien ne se fait bien qu'à deux. Les ha-bi-tants de la ter-re, Ma foi

d'el-le vient se rendre, Tout s'a-nime à l'en-tour d'eux. Et    after 2.    Danse.
ne du-re-raient guère, S'ils ne disaient pas entre eux: Et    repeat    Piccolo, Oboe, Vl. 1 and 2 in unis.
                                                          Refrain
                                                          to §,
                                                          then:    Vla.
                                                                   Bassoon    à demi-jeux
                                                          Vlc., Db.B.

Vl.2    unis./Vla.
Vla.    Vla.

Vl.1,2 unis.
Vl.2    Vla.
Vla.

§   Vl.1                                                  Piccolo, Oboe    §
Vl.2                                                      Vl.1
Vla.                                                      unis.

269

# 307. Luigi Boccherini (1743-1805)

Opus XXVII, No. 3
Minuetto

Quartet
For Strings

D.C. il Minuetto

## 308. Manuel Blasco de Nebra (*c.*1750-1784)

Opus I, No. 5
Second Movement

Sonata
For Harpsichord or Pianoforte

## 309. Samuel Webbe (1740-1816)

a. Glorious Apollo

Glee

Glo-rious A- pol- lo from on high be- held us, Wan-d'ring to find a temple for his praise, Sent Po-ly- hym-nia hith- er to

shield us, While we our- selves such a structure might raise, Thus then com- bin-ing, Hands and hearts join- ing Sing we in

har-mo-ny, A-pol-lo's praise praise, A-pol-lo's praise, A-pol-lo's praise, A-praise Here ev-'ry gen-'rous sen-ti-ment a-

wa-king, Mu-sic in-spi-ring u-ni-ty and joy Each social pleasure giving and par-taking, Glee and good humour our

hours em-ploy Then thus com-bining Hands and hearts joining Long may con-ti-nue our u-ni-ty and joy joy, our

u-ni-ty and joy our u-ni-ty and joy our u-ni-ty and joy our u-ni-ty and joy.

## b. Hot Cross Buns

Catch

al Costume. Street Cry on Good Friday.

1. Hot Cross Buns one a Pen-ny Buns two a Pen-ny

2. one a Pen-ny two a Penny hot Cross Buns one a Penny two a Penny hot Cross Buns hot Cross

3. Buns one a Penny two a Pen-ny hot Cross Buns one a Penny two a Penny Buns

4. one a Pen-ny two a Penny hot Cross Buns hot Cross Buns hot Cross Buns hot Cross Buns

5. hot Cross Buns hot Cross Buns hot Cross Buns one a Penny two a Penny hot Cross Buns.

## 310. Francis Hopkinson (1737-1791)

Beneath a weeping willow's shade

COMMENTARY AND TRANSLATIONS

# COMMENTARY

## ABBREVIATIONS

| | | |
|---|---|---|
| AS | · | *L'Anthologie Sonore* (Paris [n.d.]) |
| BuMBE | · | M. F. Bukofzer, *Music in the Baroque Era* (New York [1947]) |
| Class | · | *I Classici della musica italiana* (Milan, 1919), nos. 1–36 |
| DdT | · | *Denkmäler deutscher Tonkunst*, 65 vols. (Leipzig, 1892–1931) |
| DTB | · | *Denkmäler der Tonkunst in Bayern*, 36 vols. (Leipzig, 1900–1913) |
| DTOe | · | *Denkmäler der Tonkunst in Oesterreich*, 83 vols. (Leipzig, 1894–    ) |
| GrSHO | · | D. J. Grout, *A Short History of Opera*, 2 vols. (New York, 1947) |
| GSE | · | *The Gramaphone Shop Encyclopedia of Recorded Music* (New York, 1942) |
| HDM | · | W. Apel, *Harvard Dictionary of Music* (Cambridge, 1944) |
| Org | · | *Organum, Vierte Reihe (Orgelmusik)*, edited by M. Seiffert (Leipzig, 1923–    ) |
| TaAM | · | G. Tagliapietra, *Antologia di musica antica e moderna per il pianoforte*, 18 vols. (Milan, 1934) |
| Was | · | J. W. von Wasielewski, *Instrumentalsätze vom Ende des XVI. bis Ende des XVII. Jahrhunderts* (Berlin, 1874, 1905) |

182. JACOPO PERI: "Funeste piaggi." Peri's opera *Euridice*, performed in 1600 at Florence, appears as the first full embodiment of the novel principles of *nuove musiche*, principles which resulted from the attempts of the Florentine *camerata* to revive the drama of ancient Greece. Seven years after the production of *Euridice*, Monteverdi summarized these principles in the famous words: "L'orazione sia padrone dell' armonia e non serva" (The words should be the master, not the servant, of the music). The musical realization of this basic idea was found in the so-called monody, that is, a solo song in the character of a recitative with a simple accompaniment of sustained chords indicated by the bass notes only (*basso continuo*). Although the almost exclusive use of this style for an entire opera is an artistic misconception, Peri's recitative as such is remarkable for its archaic flavor and impressive declamation. See *GrSHO*, pp. 51ff. ¶ Sources: J. Peri, *Le musiche . . . sopra L'Euridice* (Florence, 1600), p. 14; L. Torchi, *L'Arte musicale in Italia* (Milan, 1897–1903), VI, 71; *Class*, no. 24, quad. 95, p. 14. ¶ *Record: V–21752.*

183. EMILIO DE' CAVALIERI: "A questi suoni." Cavalieri's *Rappresentazione di anima e di corpo* (Representation of Soul and Body), performed in 1600 at Rome, may best be described as a "sacred opera," a later example of which exists in Landi's *Il San Alessio* (see Nos. 208, 209). The *Rappresentazione* was produced with splendid costumes, ballet, and elaborate stage settings, such as the simultaneous representation of Hell, Earth, and Heaven at three levels. "Created for the Jesuits, it was one of the many attempts of the counter-reformation to salvage from secular art forms all those features that lent themselves to the promotion of the *ecclesia militans*" (*BuMBE*, p. 57). Through its subject matter it is related to the later oratorio (see No. 207), of which it is often considered to be the first example. In the recitative as well as in the choral sections Cavalieri employs a somewhat facile and graceless style which is inferior to that of Peri's opera. ¶ Sources: E. Cavalieri, *Rappresentazione di anima e di corpo* (Florence, 1600); facsimile edition by F. Mantica in *Prime fioriture del melodramma italiano* (Rome, 1912), I, xiv; *Class*, no. 10, quad. 35, p. 26.

184. GIULIO CACCINI: "Sfogava con le stelle." Caccini is best known as the author of *Euridice*, composed in the same year as Peri's opera of the same name and very similar. He is more important, however, as the author of *Nuove musiche* (1601), containing compositions in which for the first time the new monodic style was applied to lyrical poems. In this collection Caccini distinguishes between "arias" and "madrigals," using the former term for strophic songs, the latter for the more elaborate through-composed pieces. While Caccini's "aria" survived mainly in the German *Arien* and *Lieder* of the seventeenth century (see Nos. 205, 228), his "madrigals" became the point of departure for the Italian aria and chamber cantata (see No. 203). ¶ Sources: G. Caccini, *Le nuove musiche* (Florence, 1601), p. 13; *Class*, no. 4, quad. 10, p. 11.

185. LODOVICO GROSSI VIADANA: "Exaudi me, Domine." Viadana's reputation as the inventor of the *basso continuo* is dubious, since his *Concerti ecclesiastici* did not appear until 1602, although he claimed that they had been performed in Rome five or six years before (see the article "Thorough-bass" in Grove's *Dictionary of Music*). The chief historical significance of his *Concerti* lies in the fact that

they are the first examples of the Baroque motet with its emphasis on solo voice-parts and instrumental participation. It is this contrast of different performing bodies that the term "concerto" refers to. Noteworthy is the individual design of the bass part, resulting in a typically Baroque even weighting of the highest and lowest voices. ¶ Sources: L. G. Viadana, *Cento concerti ecclesiastici* (Venice, 1602); M. Schneider, *Die Anfänge des Basso continuo* (Leipzig, 1918), p. 172.

186. ADRIANO BANCHIERI: "Il zapaione musicale." Banchieri was born and lived in Bologna where he founded the *Accademia de' filomusi*. Many of his compositions show his predilection for comical and bizarre effects or subjects. In our selection (composed 1604), a lively, dramatic madrigal style is used to characterize a group of gay singers gathered around a bowl of punch (*zapaione*). This piece may be considered an example of the type known as madrigal comedy. ¶ Source: A. Banchieri, *Inventione boscareccia e primo libro di madrigali* (1604; manuscript copy of A. Einstein).

187, 188, 189. CLAUDIO MONTEVERDI: "Ma che temi," "Ohimè, se tanto amate," and "Non schivar, non parar." No. 187, taken from Monteverdi's first opera, *Orfeo* (1607), displays the profound poignancy of which Monteverdi was capable when dealing with the solo voice. Here the flexibility and expressiveness of the melodic line are accompanied by striking harmonic effects, often chromatic, often involving dissonance between the vocal and instrumental parts. All this, however, is not by way of abstract musical effect, but is, in each case, intended to characterize the text with dramatic intensity. No. 188 represents the culmination of the madrigalian art in Italy. The type of vocality and of chromaticism which had, at times, reached a point where instrumental participation cannot reasonably be doubted is reduced in Monteverdi to pure vocal practice. Characteristic of the composer are the repeated notes used for emphasis and for dramatic effect, and the unprepared dissonances. No. 189 demonstrates Monteverdi's departure from the accepted, contemporary approach to the writing of dramatic music in its use of the *stilo concitato* (agitated style). The overwhelming power of this scene alone entitles Monteverdi to a position among the greatest dramatic composers. Among details to be noted is the use of the tremolo and the pizzicato—perhaps the earliest dramatic occurrence of these instrumental devices. ¶ Sources: (187) C. Monteverdi, *L'Orfeo, favola in musica* (Venice, 1609), act IV; *Monteverdi's Orfeo, Facsimile des Erstdrucks der Musik*, edited by A. Sandberger (Augsburg, 1927), p. 80; *Tutte l'opere di Claudio Monteverdi*, edited by G. F. Malipiero, XI (Asolo, 1930), 124. (188) C. Monteverdi, *Il quarto libro de madrigali* (Venice, 1615); Malipiero edition (see No. 187), IV (1927), 54. (189) C. Monteverdi, *Madrigali guerrieri et amorosi, libro ottavo* (Venice, 1637); L. Torchi, *L'Arte musicale in Italia* (Milan, 1897–1903), VI, 151; *Class,* no. 19, quad. 224, p. 13; Malipiero edition (see No. 187), VIII (1929), p. 139.

190. VATER UNSER IM HIMMELREICH. The chorale prelude represents one of the most beautiful flowerings of German Baroque music. On the basis of the Roman Catholic organ hymn of the sixteenth century (Schlick, Redford, Cabezon; see Nos. 100, 101, 120, 133) there developed a tradition of organ elaborations of Protestant chorales to which most of the Baroque composers in North and Middle Germany contributed. Our four examples illustrate this development. They also afford a bird's-eye view of the stylistic evolution from Scheidt to Bach. ¶ Sources: (a) S. Scheidt, *Tabulatura nova* (Halle, 1624); *DdT*, I, 16. (b) *Buxtehude, Orgelkompositionen*, edited by P. Spitta, revised edition by M. Seiffert (Leipzig, 1903–04), Choralbearbeitungen, Abteilung II, no. 9b. (c) F. Commer, *Meister des Orgelbarock*, revised edition by H. F. Redlich (Berlin, 1931), p. 58. (d) *J. S. Bach's Compositionen für die Orgel* (Leipzig: C. F. Peters (187?–192?)), V, 52. ¶ Records: (b) *G–DB5260;* (c) *AS–10* (*GSE*, p. 335); (d) *VM–711.*

191. GIOVANNI MARIA TRABACI: "Canzona francese." Trabaci was a member of an interesting, though little-known, school of keyboard composers that flourished in Naples before and after 1600. Connected in various ways with Cabezon, they are even more important as predecessors of Frescobaldi. Our canzona consists of five sections, alternating between duple and triple meter, each of which is a short fugal elaboration of the same theme. Thus it is an early example of the variation canzona which was extensively cultivated by Frescobaldi (see *BuMBE*, p. 50). The identity of the first and last sections should also be noticed (cyclical treatment; see *HDM*, p. 197; for a later example see No. 210). ¶ Source: G. M. Trabaci, *Ricercate, canzone francese, capricci* . . . (Naples, 1603), p. 53.

192. GIROLAMO FRESCOBALDI: "Partite sopra l'aria della Romanesca." Frescobaldi, organist at St. Peter's in Rome, represents the consummation of Baroque organ music in Italy. The Romanesca melody, which was used by numerous early Baroque composers as a theme for variations (see also No. 199), is almost identical with that of the sixteenth-century Spanish "Guardame las vacas" (see No. 124) and of the *passamezzo antico* (see No. 154). This similarity is most apparent when the bass lines are compared (see *BuMBE*, p. 41). In the original source the composition is barred in 4/2, as indicated at the beginning of our reproduction. This is one of the many examples of the period where the true meter of the composition is obscured by the original time signature and bar lines (see No. 199). The small notes added at the beginning of "Quinta parte" and elsewhere indicate original note values. ¶ Sources: G. Frescobaldi, *Toccate d'intavolatura di cimbalo et organo* . . . (Rome, 1637), p. 41; O. Chilesotti, *Biblioteca di rarità musicali* (Milan [1885?–1915?]), VI, 1; *TaAM*, IV, 20.

193. GIROLAMO FRESCOBALDI: "Toccata." The toccata, which Claudio Merulo had treated in a form and style of imposing breadth and self-assurance (see No. 153), completely changed its character in the hands of Frescobaldi. Nowhere in music is the frenzied restlessness of the early Baroque period more clearly illustrated than in his toccatas,

with their disintegrated structure, their multiplicity of formations, their jerky motives, bold syncopations, and complicated cross rhythms. The strange "meters," 8/12, 4/6, and so on, which occur in this composition are explained as remnants of the proportional system of the fifteenth and sixteenth centuries. In reality, these signs are not metrical but temporal indications signifying the relationship of note values; for example, 12 notes in the subsequent section as being equivalent to 8 in the preceding one. To notice this is all the more important because it also applies to the familiar looking signs 12/8, 6/4, 3/2 of this composition and others of the period. Not until after 1650 was the proportional (that is, temporal) meaning of these signs replaced by the metrical significance (kind and number of notes to the measure) they have today. ¶ Sources: G. Frescobaldi, *Il secondo libro di toccate* . . . (Rome, 1637), p. 26; F. Boghen, *Antichi maestri italiani: toccate* (Milan, 1918), p. 43; *TaAM*, v, 24.

194. GIROLAMO FRESCOBALDI: "Canzona." Like Trabaci's organ canzona (see No. 191), this canzona by Frescobaldi consists of several short fugal sections. The variation principle, however, and the cyclical treatment encountered there are not used here. A typically Frescobaldian trait is the free cadential ending, which often serves to retard the motion as if under the impact of powerful brakes. ¶ Sources: G. Frescobaldi, *Il secondo libro di toccate* . . . (Rome, 1637), p. 53; *Hieronymus Frescobaldi, Ausgewählte Orgelsätze,* edited by F. X. Haberl (Leipzig [191?]), II, 22.

195. HEINRICH SCHEIDEMANN: "Praeludium." Scheidemann, who was active in Hamburg, was an early member of the North German school which culminated in Buxtehude. His organ preludes are interesting because they indicate the point of departure of one of the most important forms of the late Baroque period, the prelude and fugue. While the first of our two preludes contains just a short point of imitation, the second actually is a prelude followed by a fugue. ¶ Source: *Org,* no. 8, pp. 4, 16.

196. SAMUEL SCHEIDT: "Wehe, Windgen, wehe." Samuel Scheidt, who worked in Halle, was, like Scheidemann, a pupil of Sweelinck (see also the remark under No. 181). His *Tabulatura nova* of 1624 is the most important document of German organ music in the early Baroque period. The variations of our example are all of the *cantus firmus* type, except variation 2 which is figural (see *BuMBE,* pp. 105f). ¶ Sources: S. Scheidt, *Tabulatura nova* (Halle, 1624); *DdT,* I, 51.

197. JOHANN HERMANN SCHEIN: "Intrada." Schein, Scheidt, and Schütz form a famous trio of German "Sch"-composers born around 1585. From 1615 until his death, Schein held the post of cantor at St. Thomas' in Leipzig, which was later occupied by J. S. Bach. Schein is equally important in the field of vocal and of instrumental ensemble music (see *BuMBE,* pp. 85f). His *Banchetto musicale* of 1617, from which this selection is taken, stands at the beginning of German instrumental music. It contains suites consisting of Paduana, Gaillarde, Courante, Allemande, and Tripla. Our Intrada, which is added separately at the end of the collection, is interesting for its specification of instruments. The *cornett* should not be confused with the modern cornet (see the articles in *HDM*). ¶ Sources: J. Schein, *Banchetto musicale* (Leipzig, 1617); *Johann Hermann Schein, Sämtliche Werke,* edited by A. Prüfer, I (Leipzig, 1901), 198.

198. GIOVANNI BATTISTA FONTANA: "Sonata." This example illustrates the transition from the *canzona da sonar* to the sonata. The new name referred not so much to a new form (which did not evolve until later), but to a new style and texture; the many-voiced and fugal writing of the canzona being replaced by the characteristic *continuo* style (two outer voices with filled-in harmonies) of the Baroque era (see *BuMBE,* pp. 51f). The emergence of the violin as a solo instrument played an important part in this evolution. ¶ Sources: G. B. Fontana, *Sonate a uno, due, tre per il violino o cornetto, fagotto, chitarone, violoncino o simile altro instrumento* (Venice, 1641); D. J. Iselin, *Biagio Marini* (Hildburghausen, 1930), example 13.

199. BIAGIO MARINI: "Romanesca." Marini, probably a pupil of Fontana, was born and was active in Brescia, the place of the earliest makers of violins (Gasparo da Salò and G. P. Maggini). He also worked in Venice, Parma, and Düsseldorf. His Romanesca variations (published in 1620) are based on the same theme used by Frescobaldi (see No. 192). In our rendition the original barring has been retained, and the intended grouping in triple measures has been indicated underneath. ¶ Sources: B. Marini, *Arie madrigali et corenti* . . . (Venice, 1620); *Was,* no. x.

200. MANUEL RODRIGUES COELHO: "Verso do primeiro tom." Coelho is one of the few known representatives of seventeenth-century Portuguese music. He was organist of the cathedrals of Elvas and Lisbon. His *Flores de musica* of 1620 includes a collection of "Versos," that is, versets for the Psalms and the Magnificat, such as were written by many composers before and after him (see Nos. 133, 251). While these versets are usually for organ, Coelho writes them for the organ and a voice part (to be sung, no doubt, by the organist himself), in the manner of Viadana's *Concerti ecclesiastici* (see No. 185). ¶ Source: M. R. Coelho, *Flores de musica* (Lisbon, 1620), p. 174.

201. HEINRICH SCHÜTZ: "Da Jesus an dem Kreuze stund" and "Und um die neunte Stunde." (a) The opening chorus of the *Seven Last Words* represents a combination of German devoutness as expressed in the simple, often chordal writing, and of harmonic and chromatic subtlety which reflects Schütz's Italian experience. To this must be added, of course, the quality, not to be analyzed, of Schütz's own particular eloquence. (b) Before Schütz it was generally the custom to set the words of our Lord for four voices. Here the composer markedly emphasizes the personal quality of

the text by assigning it to a single voice. In this, as in other particulars, Schütz prefigures his successor, J. S. Bach. ¶ Sources: (a) *Heinrich Schütz, Sämtliche Werke,* edited by P. Spitta (Leipzig, 1885), I, 147; H. Schütz, *Die Sieben Worte Jesu Christi am Kreuz* . . . edited by Dr. F. Stein, Eulenburg's Kleine Partitur-Ausgabe no. 977 (Leipzig [1934]), p. 1. (b) Spitta edition (see 201a), I, 152; Eulenburg's Kleine Partitur-Ausgabe no. 977 (see 201b), p. 11.

202. HEINRICH SCHÜTZ: "Saul, Saul." Schütz's dramatic power is forcefully displayed in this selection, remarkable not only in the age in which it was composed but worthy of genius in any period. Whereas in earlier times emphasis on some features of the text was generally achieved by the use of repeated notes or chords, here the word "Saul" is reiterated in successively higher groupings or is passed about among the choirs with almost feverish insistence. The technique and the texture are clearly referable to the style of Giovanni Gabrieli, with whom Schütz studied; but the fervor of the expression is all German. ¶ Sources: H. Schütz, *Symphoniarum sacrarum tertia pars,* op. 12 (Dresden, 1650); Spitta edition (see No. 201), XI, 99. ¶ Record: *G–EJ250.*

203. LUIGI ROSSI: "Io·lo vedo." Rossi was active mainly in the field of the cantata. In fact, he may be said to have created it by expanding the aria (madrigal) of the early monodists (see No. 184) into a composite form including recitatives, ariosos, and arias (see *BuMBE,* p. 120). He also was one of the first to cultivate the *da capo* form of the aria, A B A, a form which was universally adopted in the late Baroque period (see Nos. 244 and 258). Our selection is an example of this form. ¶ Source: Brussels, Bibliothèque Royale, *MS 2422* (manuscript copy of A. Einstein).

204. HENRY LAWES: "Sweet Echo." Lawes, who was a gentleman of the Chapel Royal of London, is mainly remembered for his music to Milton's masque *Comus,* performed in 1634. The masque, the forerunner of the English opera, was a dramatic entertainment accompanied by elaborate scenery and by singing and dancing (see *GrSHO,* pp. 133f). Lawes largely abandoned the tradition of the English madrigal style; he was concerned, rather, with a faithful setting of the text "with just note and accent" (see *HDM,* p. 385), and his care in this regard made him a favorite with contemporary English poets. Both the melody and the accompaniment of our selection suggest not a little the methods of the *nuove musiche* (see Nos. 182ff). ¶ Sources: London, British Museum, *Add. MS 11518;* J. Hawkins, *General History of Science and Practice of Music,* IV (London, 1776), 53; C. Burney, *A General History of Music* (London, 1776–1789), III, 383; *The Masque of Comus,* edited by Sir F. Bridge (London [1908]), p. 38.

205. HEINRICH ALBERT: "Auf, mein Geist." Albert, a cousin of Schütz, was organist at Königsberg in East Prussia (now Russia). His "arias" occupy a prominent position in the development of the Baroque *Lied* because they represent the transition from the mere imitation of the Italian monody to a truly German type of song, characterized by an ardent expression of devout feelings. Also typical is the use of an instrumental ritornello ("Symphonia"). ¶ Source: *DdT,* XII, 11.

206. FRANCESCO CAVALLI: "Ecco la lettra." Cavalli, a pupil of Monteverdi, is associated with the rise of the Venetian opera (see *GrSHO,* pp. 84ff). His operas, written for the first public opera house—founded in Venice, 1637—and performed in Vienna and Paris, are characterized by many novel features, such as lavish stage production, complete abandoning of the chorus, extensive use of the aria, often in tuneful and dance-like melodies, and introduction of the *recitativo secco,* that is, a recitative of a dry, speech-like character designed for a narrative or a dialogue and accompanied by sustained chords played on the harpsichord (for other types of Baroque recitative see Nos. 182, 187, 201, 225, 255, and 281). Our selection from *Xerxes* (*Serse,* 1654) shows the usual combination of a recitative and an aria. ¶ Source: F. Cavalli, *Xerxes* (1654; manuscript copy in the Library of Congress), act II, scene viii.

207. GIACOMO CARISSIMI: "Miserunt ergo sortem." Carissimi was active in Tivoli, Assisi, and, from about 1628, in Rome. While seventeenth-century Italian composers were, in the main, busy with the writing of opera, Carissimi devoted himself to the oratorio, which afforded him the opportunity to indulge his particular talent for choral writing; for, while over a considerable period the opera and oratorio employed many features in common, the oratorio came to lay much greater emphasis on the chorus than did the opera. The use of the repeated note found in the chorus was employed by both Peri and Caccini in their *Euridice*'s; it generally suggests a concentration on the import of the text. ¶ Source: *Carissimi's Werke,* edited by F. Chrysander, Denkmäler der Tonkunst (Bergedorf [187?]), I, 105.

208, 209. STEFFANO LANDI: "Sinfonia" and "Poca voglia di far bene." Landi is the main representative of the Roman school of opera which flourished from about 1620 to 1640, following the Florentine opera and preceding that of Venice (see *GrSHO,* pp. 70ff). His *Il San Alessio* (1632) is a characteristically Roman opera in its use of a sacred story for its plot (the libretto was written by the Marchese Rospigliosi, who later became Pope Clement IX), of choruses which largely replaced the recitative of the Florentine operas, and of comic scenes such as the charming duet of two lazy and light-headed pages which is reproduced here. The two "Sinfonias" of *Il San Alessio,* one for each act, are unusually extended and developed for their time. Moreover, they both are instrumental canzonas in three sections, fast-slow-fast, thus anticipating the characteristic three-movement form of the later Neapolitan sinfonia (Italian overture; see No. 259). In No. 209 the figures over the bass in the first measure of the two-measure repeat section occur only the second time in the score. ¶ Sources: (208) F. Landi, *Il San Alessio* (Rome, 1634), act II;

H. Goldschmidt, *Studien zur Geschichte der italienischen Oper,* I (Leipzig, 1901), 252. (209) F. Landi, *Il San Alessio* (Rome, 1634), act I, scene iii; Goldschmidt (see No. 208), I, 210.

**210. TARQUINIO MERULA:** "Canzon detta la Vesconta." Although originally designated as "canzona," this composition may well be called a sonata (see remark under No. 198). In fact, it can be considered an early example of the trio sonata which came into prominence toward the end of the seventeenth century (see Nos. 245, 269; also *BuMBE,* p. 53). The similarity of the first and last sections should be noticed (cyclical treatment; see *HDM,* p. 197; for an earlier example, see No. 191). ¶ Sources: T. Merula, *Il secondo libro delle canzoni da suonare a tre . . .* (Venice, 1639); *Was,* no. XVII.

**211. DENIS GAULTIER:** "Mode sous-ionien." Denis Gaultier was the most famous member of a family of French lutenists. He developed a highly idiomatic lute style of great subtlety and flexibility which exercised a decisive influence on the harpsichord style of Froberger (see No. 216) and of the French clavecinists (see No. 232). Our selection is taken from a sumptuous manuscript collection of Gaultier's works, *La Rhétorique des dieux,* in which stylized dances are arranged according to keys (regarding the meaning of "sous-ionien" see *HDM,* p. 147; see also *BuMBE,* pp. 164ff). In a later publication by Perrine (*Livre de musique pour le luth,* 1679) our piece appears in an interesting modification, with dotted rhythms and lute ornaments, as indicated for the beginning of our reproduction. ¶ Sources: Berlin, Kupferstich-kabinett, *Codex Hamilton* ("La Rhétorique des dieux"); Perrine, *Livre de musique pour le luth* (Paris, 1679), p. 165; O. Fleischer, *Denis Gaultier* (Leipzig, 1889), p. 165; *La Rhétorique des dieux . . .* edited by A. Tessier (Paris, 1932–33), p. 60.

**212. JACQUES CHAMPION DE CHAMBONNIÈRES:** "Chaconne." Chambonnières is the first in the series of French clavecinists (*clavecin,* in other words, harpsichord). He worked at Versailles, as court musician to Louis XIV (see *BuMBE,* p. 170). His chaconne is not in the traditional form of continuous variations, but in that of the rondeau, as are most of the chaconnes of the French clavecinists (see also No. 240). ¶ Sources: Paris, Bibliothèque nationale, *MS Bauyn* (c. 1650); *Oeuvres complètes de Chambonnières,* edited by P. Brunold and A. Tessier (Paris, 1925), p. 92. ¶ Records: *V–15186* and *DB–4973.*

**213. ANDREAS HAMMERSCHMIDT:** "Wende dich, Herr." The quasi-dramatic form of the dialogue was widely cultivated by composers in the seventeenth century (see No. 226). The solemn tones of the trombone form an impressive contrast to the flexibility of the vocal lines which emphasize the petitioning character of the text. ¶ Sources: A. Hammerschmidt, *Dialogi oder Gespräche zwischen Gott und einer gläubigen Seele,* Erster Theil (Dresden, 1645); *DTOe,* VIII(1), 131.

**214, 215. FRANZ TUNDER:** "Wachet auf" and "Praeludium." Tunder was organist of the Marienkirche at Lübeck, where he was succeeded by his son-in-law, Buxtehude (see No. 234). Of particular importance are Tunder's chorale compositions, either for the organ (chorale prelude) or for voices (chorale cantata). The present example (No. 214) is a chorale cantata for solo voice, consisting of a short "Sinfonia," a full presentation of the chorale, and a concluding section (3/4) in which various motives of the chorale melody are developed. The "Praeludium" (No. 215) actually is a prelude, fugue, and postlude (see No. 195). ¶ Sources: (214) *DdT,* III, 107. (215) *Org,* no. 6, p. 3.

**216, 217. JOHANN JACOB FROBERGER:** "Lamento" and "Toccata II." Froberger holds a central position in the evolution of Baroque keyboard music. Born in Stuttgart, he studied in Rome under Frescobaldi, was organist in Vienna, visited Brussels, Paris, and London, and died at the castle of the Duchess Sybil of Würthemberg at Héricourt. This cosmopolitanism is clearly reflected in his compositions, which are a happy amalgamation of German, French, and Italian elements. The "Lamento sopra la dolorosa perdita della Real Maestà di Ferdinando IV," one of the most impressive embodiments of the "Romantic" current in Baroque music, is the first movement (Allemande) of a suite in C. The toccata, although lacking the boldness and intensity of Frescobaldi's tonal language, shows an advance in the direction of organization, formal as well as melodic and harmonic (see *BuMBE,* pp. 108ff). ¶ Sources: (216) Vienna, Staatsbibliothek, *autograph MS; DTOe,* VI(2), 32; *TaAM,* VI, 142. (217) Vienna, Staatsbibliothek, *autograph MS; DTOe,* IV(1), 5; *Early Keyboard Music,* edited by L. Oesterle (New York, 1904), I, 67; *TaAM,* VI, 111.

**218. JOHANN ROSENMÜLLER:** "Aleph. Ego vir." Rosenmüller, born in Saxony, spent part of his restless and adventurous life in Leipzig, Hamburg, and Venice. His musical output comprises important instrumental works as well as vocal compositions. Scheibe, the music critic of the Bach period, placed him side by side with Lully, saying that "he put almost the whole of Italy to shame." A characteristic feature of the "Lamentations" is the use of Hebrew letters for the enumeration of the verses. Baroque composers usually treated each of these letters as an expressive vocal melisma. ¶ Sources: Berlin, Preussische Staatsbibliothek, music *MS 18883; Nagel's Musik Archiv,* no. 28 (Hanover, 1929), p. 8.

**219. MAURIZIO CAZZATI:** "Sonata prima La Pellicana." Cazzati is one of the early members of the Bologna school of instrumental music which also included G. B. Vitali and G. Torelli (see Nos. 245, 246). The Bolognese composers worked in the direction of a refined formalism, avoiding the exuberance and virtuosity of the early violinists like Fontana and Marini (see Nos. 198, 199). The frequent use of imitation between the upper part and the bass may be noticed in our example. ¶ Source: M. Cazzati, *Sonate a due instrumenti cioe violino e violone* . . . op. 55 (Bologna, 1670; manuscript copy of H. Mishkin).

220. GIOVANNI LEGRENZI: "La Buscha." Legrenzi is the main representative of the Venetian school of instrumental music (see *BuMBE*, pp. 137f). The heritage of Giovanni Gabrieli is clearly apparent in the full orchestral texture and in the polychoral elements of this extremely interesting sonata. ¶ Source: G. Legrenzi, *Sonate a due, tre, cinque, e sei stromenti*, op. VIII (Bologna, 1671; manuscript copy of A. Einstein).

221. MARC' ANTONIO CESTI: "Di bellezza e di valore." Cesti is the main representative of the second generation of the Venetian operatic school (see No. 206). His rising fame threatened to eclipse the success of the aging Cavalli, particularly after the eminently successful performance of *La Dori* (1661) and of *Il pomo d'oro*. The latter, composed for the wedding of the Austrian Emperor Leopold I and performed in Vienna in 1667, was a festival show piece on a grandiose scale, including several ballets and requiring twenty-four stage settings with highly elaborate machines. Compared to Cavalli's, Cesti's music is less vigorous and dramatic, more lyrical, and occasionally facile (see *GrSHO*, pp. 95ff). ¶ Sources: M. A. Cesti, *Il pomo d'oro* (1668), act IV, scene xii; *DTOe*, IV(2), 173.

222. FRANCESCO PROVENZALE: "Lasciatemi morir." Provenzale may be regarded as the founder of the Neapolitan school of opera which held first place throughout the late Baroque period (see *GrSHO*, pp. 179ff). Unfortunately, his work has been almost completely neglected by modern research. His *Il schiavo di sua moglie* (The Slave of His Wife, 1671) is a humorous opera, but retains the dignified style of the serious opera. Our selection is an example of the *ostinato* aria, widely used by the earlier Baroque composers, in which the bass repeats a fixed melodic formula (ground bass). It also illustrates the expressive *bel canto* style which is characteristic of the Neapolitan school. The accompaniment is probably for a three-voice string orchestra. ¶ Sources: F. Provenzale, *Il schiavo di sua moglie* (manuscript copy in the Library of Congress), act I, scene viii; Romain Rolland, *Histoire de l'opéra en Europe avant Lully et Scarlatti*, new edition by E. de Boccard (Paris, 1931), supplément musicale, p. 9.

223. ROBERT CAMBERT: "Overture to *Pomone*." *Pomone* (1671) was the first French opera really deserving this name (see *BuMBE*, p. 150). In the overture to this opera we find the essential stylistic elements of the French overture, a slow introduction of a pompous character with dotted rhythms, to be followed by a fast section in fugal style. ¶ Sources: R. Cambert, *Pomone* (Paris, 1671; lost? Manuscript copy in Paris, Conservatoire de musique); *Cambert, Pomone*, edited by J. B. Wekerlin, Chefs-d'oeuvre de l'opéra française (Paris [1880?]), p. 1; E. M. E. Deldevez, *Pièces*

diverses choisies dans les oeuvres des célèbres compositeurs . . . (Paris [1880?]), p. 31.

224, 225. JEAN–BAPTISTE LULLY: "Overture" and "Le Ciel protège les héros." Lully, born in Florence, came to France in 1646 and produced his first opera in 1672, after an extensive activity mostly in the field of ballet music. *Alceste*, his first master opera, was composed in 1674. Lully established a national type of aristocratic opera which was for many years the model which French composers followed (see *BuMBE*, pp. 151ff; *GrSHO*, pp. 116ff). He established, in particular, the form and style of the so-called French overture (see No. 223). Sometimes he expanded this into a three-sectional form, by stating the first idea, or one of a similar character, in a concluding section. The recitative in our vocal selection is also characteristic of Lully's method, the chief aim being utmost fidelity to proper text accentuation. This often leads to the employment of mixed meters. ¶ Sources: (224) J. B. Lully, *Alceste* (Paris, 1674); *Oeuvres complètes de J.–B. Lully, les opéras*, vol. II, *Alceste*, edited by H. Prunières (Paris, 1932), p. 9. (225) J. B. Lully, *Alceste* (Paris, 1674), act I, scene ix; *Alceste*, Prunières edition (see No. 224), p. 101. ¶ Record: (224) *V-7424*.

226. MARC ANTOINE CHARPENTIER: "Dialogue entre Madeleine et Jésus." Charpentier was a pupil of Carissimi (see No. 207), a fact which accounts for the Italian traits in his music and for his extensive cultivation of the oratorio. It is curious to notice that the Frenchman Charpentier championed the Italian style at the same time that the Italian Lully made himself the protagonist of French taste. Our selection is taken from Charpentier's masterpiece, the oratorio *Le Reniement de St-Pierre* (see *BuMBE*, pp. 161ff). ¶ Source: M. A. Charpentier, *Le Reniement de St. Pierre*, livraison III of C. Bordes, Concerts spirituels (Bureau d'édition de la Schola Cantorum [1901?–1905?]), p. 1.

227. JOAN CEREROLS: "Señor mio Jesu Cristo." The Palestrina style of church composition was perpetuated in Spain by several composers—among them Cererols, who belonged to a musical school domiciled at the monastery of Montserrat in the Pyrenees. The *villancico*, a type of half-secular, half-religious poetry, which had been cultivated since the thirteenth century in various musical styles (see Nos. 22, 97, 98), came to new life in the seventeenth century in what may be termed the Spanish counterpart of the church cantata. Very often these *villancicos* both open and close with a choral movement called *estribillo*, between which there are one or more solo numbers, the *coplas*. ¶ Source: D. Pujol, *Mestres de l'escolania de Montserrat*, vol. III (Monastery of Montserrat, 1903), pt. 3, p. 48.

228. ADAM KRIEGER: "Adonis Tod." Krieger, a pupil of Scheidt, worked in Leipzig and Dresden, where he died at the age of thirty-two. He is, together with Erlebach (see No. 254), the outstanding representative of the German Baroque *Lied* (see No. 205). Combining the Italian *bel canto*

with a German feeling for strength and sincerity, he composed a large number of impressive songs, lyrical as well as humorous. His preferred form was that of the strophic song with instrumental ritornellos. ¶ Sources: A. Krieger, *Neue Arien* (Dresden, 1676); *DdT*, XIX, 16.

229. LOUIS COUPERIN: "Menuet de Poitou." Louis Couperin, uncle of François Couperin (see Nos. 265, 266), was one of the numerous pupils of Chambonnières (see No. 212). His minuets are among the earliest examples of a dance which was to be of such lasting importance in the history of music. This piece shows the three-measure phrases which are characteristic of the early minuet. ¶ Sources: Paris, Bibliothèque nationale, *MS Bauyn* (see No. 212); *Oeuvres complètes de Louis Couperin*, edited by P. Brunold (Paris, 1936), p. 140.

230. MATTHEW LOCKE: "Fantazia." Locke's *Consort of ffoure Parts* contains six suites, each consisting of a Fantazia, Courante, Ayre, and Sarabande. The first movement of the sixth suite, reproduced here, shows the succession of short fugal sections characteristic of the English fancy (see Morley's description in *HDM*, s.v. "Fancy"). ¶ Sources: London, British Museum, *autograph MS; Six String Quartets by Matthew Locke*, edited by A. Mangeot (London, 1932), no. 6 ¶ Record: *NGS-143*.

231. NICOLAS ANTOINE LE BÈGUE: "Noël, 'Une vierge pucelle.'" The French organ composers of the Baroque period were strongly influenced by the secular trends which prevailed at the court of the French kings. Catering to the demands of a pleasure-seeking society, they introduced dances and popular tunes into the service. They were the first to exploit systematically the coloristic possibilities of the organ, and to prescribe specific registrations (see *BuMBE*, p. 172). The "noëls" are popular Christmas tunes treated as variations. *P. J.* means *plein jeu, G.* means *grande orgue.* ¶ Sources: N. A. le Bègue, *Troisième livre d'orgue* (Paris [1690?]); A. Pirro, *Archives des maîtres de l'orgue*, IX (Paris, 1909), 214.

232. JEAN HENRI D'ANGLEBERT: "Prélude, Allemande, Sarabande." D'Anglebert represents the artistic culmination of the true Baroque style in French harpsichord music (see the remark under No. 265). Our selections are taken from the G-minor group of his *Pièces de clavecin*, a group which includes twenty-two numbers, many of them adaptations from the operas of Lully. The Prélude illustrates a unique type of entirely free design and rhythm which was established by Louis Couperin. Its derivation from lute music is apparent. The Allemande is remarkable for its extended flow and continued intensity. In the Sarabande the exploitation of the low registers of the harpsichord may be noticed. ¶ Sources: J. H. d'Anglebert, *Pièces de clavecin* (Paris, 1689); *Pièces de clavecin composées par J. Henry d'Anglebert*, edited by M. Rœsgen-Champion (Paris, 1934), pp. 36, 38; *TaAM*, VII, 112.

233. ESAJAS REUSNER: "Prelude." After lute music had declined in France, giving way to the popular guitar, it came to a late flowering in Germany under Reusner, and Bach's contemporary Silvius Weiss. Reusner was the first German composer to open his suites with a free prelude. ¶ Sources: *Deliciae Testudinis* (1667); H. Riemann, "Zur Geschichte der deutschen Suite," in *Sammelbände der Internationalen Musikgesellschaft* (Leipzig, 1903–04), VI, 509.

234, 235. DIETRICH BUXTEHUDE: "Praeludium cum fuga" and "Liebster Herr Jesu." Buxtehude, born in Sweden, became Tunder's successor at the Marienkirche of Lübeck, where his "Abendmusiken" (weekly concerts during Advent) attracted visitors from near and far, among them the young J. S. Bach (1705). Buxtehude represents the high point of the North German school of organ music. His "Praeludium cum fuga" is actually a toccata, consisting of several fugues preceded and followed by sections in free style, a form which was established by Merulo (see No. 153). Buxtehude brought this form to new life, filling it with a characteristically North German spirit of mysticism and unbounded exultation. His vocal music is much more conservative and often shows Italian influence. Our selection is from the cantata *Eins bitte ich vom Herrn.* This consists of an instrumental "Sonatina," a chorus, and an "Aria" of seven verses which are composed for solo voice and chorus alternately, with instrumental ritornellos at the close of each verse. ¶ Sources: (234) *Buxtehude, Orgelkompositionen* (see No. 190), I, 41. (235) *DdT*, XIV, 23.

236. ALESSANDRO POGLIETTI: "Aria allemagna con alcuni variazioni." Poglietti was an Italian who worked in Vienna, and who died there during the Turkish siege in 1683. His "Aria allemagna," written in 1677 as a birthday present for the ruling Austrian empress, represents through the number of variations (22) the age of his patroness. Many of these variations are based on programmatic ideas, which in amusing fashion portray topics from the various provinces of the sprawling Austrian empire; for example, our selections: "Alter Weiber Conduct" (Old Hag's Procession), "Französische Baiselemans" (French Kiss-the-Hand), "Polnischer Sablschertz" (Polish Swordplay [?]). ¶ Sources: *DTOe*, XIII(2), 13; *TaAM*, VIII, 1.

237. JOHANN CHRISTOPH BACH: "Praeludium und fuge ex dis." Johann Christoph Bach, an uncle of Johann Sebastian, was organist at Eisenach. His prelude and fugue in E-flat (*Dis*, that is to say, D-sharp) has been erroneously included among the works of J. S. Bach (see *Bach-Gesellschaft* (Leipzig, 1851ff), vol. XXXVI, no. 12). ¶ Source: A. G. Ritter, *Zur Geschichte des Orgelspiels* (Leipzig, 1884), II, 172.

238. HEINRICH FRANZ BIBER: "Surrexit Christus hodie." Biber, who was director of music to the archbishop of Salzburg and who was knighted by the Austrian emperor in 1690, raised the violin music of his day to an extraordinary height of technical and artistic perfection (see *BuMBE*,

p. 116). Particularly famous are his so-called "Mystery Sonatas" of about 1675, each of which represents in a general way a biblical incident. The present movement, taken from the "Resurrection Sonata" (no. XI), is a passacaglia in which the resurrection hymn "Surrexit Christus hodie" serves as a *basso ostinato* (ground). The violin part in this selection requires the use of *scordatura* (mis-tuning). The tuning for the violin indicated in the original edition is g g′ d′ d″ instead of the customary g d′ a′ e″ (see *HDM*, s.v. "Scordatura"). ¶ Source: *DTOe*, XII(2), 52 (regarding mistakes in this edition, see M. Schneider, *Zeitschrift der Internationalen Musikgesellschaft* (Leipzig, 1908), VIII, 471).

239. JUAN CABANILLES: "Paseos." Cabanilles was organist of the cathedral at Valencia in Spain. His numerous organ works show him as an ingenious master in the handling of formalistic problems, often reminiscent of Sweelinck. The *paseos* reproduced here are continuous variations (chaconne) based on a four-measure scheme of harmonies: I–I–IV–V. ¶ Source: *Johannis Cabanilles Opera omnia*, edited by H. Anglès (Barcelona, 1927), II, 120.

240. GEORG MUFFAT: "Passacaglia." Muffat was an Austrian composer who studied for six years with Lully. The present selection from his *Apparatus musico-organisticus* of 1690 shows the French influence, not only in the liberal use of ornaments but also in its formal structure. It is a passacaglia (without a ground bass), consisting of twenty-four variations which are divided into four equal sections by the regular recurrence of the original theme at the end of each section (variations 6, 12, 18, and 24). This unique form represents an amalgamation of the Italian and the French type of passacaglia (chaconne), or, in other words, of variation and rondeau (see No. 212). Our rendition has been shortened by one variation in each section. ¶ Sources: G. Muffat, *Apparatus musico-organisticus* (Augsburg, 1690); *Apparatus* . . . edited by S. de Lange (Leipzig, 1888), p. 66; *TaAM*, VIII, 60.

241. ALESSANDRO STRADELLA: "Tra cruci funeste." Stradella was a Neapolitan whose adventurous life came to a premature end when he was killed by the hirelings of a Venetian nobleman whose mistress he had abducted. Stradella is a representative of the Venetian operatic school (see Nos. 206, 221). Our selection, with its *prestissimo parlando*, is typical in its energy and conciseness. ¶ Source: A. Stradella, *Il Corispero* (c. 1665; manuscript copy in the Library of Congress), act II, scene xiv.

242. PELHAM HUMPHREY: "O Lord, my God." Humphrey's fame has, to a considerable degree, been overshadowed by that of his greater contemporary, Henry Purcell. Like Purcell, Humphrey represents the flowering of English music in the Restoration period. A pupil of Lully, Humphrey brought back to England and incorporated in his music many details of French style. Among these, and to be observed in the choral section, is the iambic meter so common in the music of Lully. The first three out of a total of five sections are given here. ¶ Sources: W. Boyce, *Cathedral Music* (London, 1788), II, 242; J. Warren, *Cathedral Music . . . Selected by Dr. William Boyce* (London, 1849), III, 229.

243. JOHN BLOW: "Mourn for thy servant." Blow's *Venus and Adonis* is the earliest extant English opera with music throughout, and serves, in many respects, as the model for *Dido and Aeneas* by Blow's pupil, Purcell (see No. 255). The first performance of *Venus and Adonis* was at the court of Charles II and probably took place no later than 1684, as the king's death occurred in the following year. The original score of our selection (final chorus), besides the continuo part, has four separate string parts, one doubling exactly each of the four voice parts. ¶ Sources: *MS* at Christ Church, Oxford; *Venus and Adonis: A Masque,* edited by G. E. P. Arkwright, The Old English Edition, xxv (London, 1902), 137; *John Blow, Venus and Adonis,* Tercentenary Edition, edited by A. Lewis (Editions de L'Oiseau Lyre; Monaco, 1949).

244. AGOSTINO STEFFANI: "Un balen." Steffani, a North Italian who spent most of his life in Germany (Munich, Hanover), was a highly successful diplomat as well as an outstanding composer. Combining his native operatic style with traits of French derivation (particularly in the overtures), he laid the foundation for the German opera of Keiser (see No. 267) and the young Handel. His music is characterized by a discipline and noble restraint which enhance, rather than impair, its expressive values. Noteworthy features of our selection are the "motto" beginning, the fully developed *da capo* form with a contrasting middle section, and the effective use of vocal coloraturas. ¶ Source: A. Steffani, *Henrico Leone* (1689: manuscript copy in the Library of Congress), act I, scene xiii.

245. GIOVANNI BATTISTA VITALI: "Sonata La Graziani." Vitali, who was a pupil of Cazzati (see No. 219), represents, together with Torelli (see No. 246), the artistic highpoint of the Bologna school of instrumental music. He was one of the first to distinguish clearly between the *sonata da chiesa* and the *sonata da camera* (see *BuMBE*, p. 139). ¶ Sources: G. B. Vitali, *Sonate a due, tre, quattro e cinque stromenti*, op. 5 (Bologna, 1669); *Was*, no. XXVII, p. 48.

246. GIUSEPPE TORELLI: "Concerto opus VIII, no. 8." Torelli, an outstanding member of the Bologna school, established the stylistic details and the form of the Baroque concerto (see *BuMBE*, pp. 226f). His opus VIII, no. 8, is a solo concerto in three movements, fast-slow-fast, with well-characterized solo sections, particularly in the last movement. ¶ Sources: G. Torelli, *Concerti grossi*, op. 8 (Bologna, 1709); *Torelli, Concerto C-moll*, edited by E. Praetorius (Leipzig, 1939).

247, 248. JOHANN KASPAR FERDINAND FISCHER: "Prelude and Fugue" and "Suite." Fischer lived in the southwestern part of Germany, and worked as court conductor to the Margrave of Baden. His *Ariadne musica* of 1715 is a collection of preludes and fugues in nearly all the keys (only five are omitted), and it is this multitude of keys—truly a labyrinth for the musicians of that day—to which the allegorical title refers. Our selection from this work shows that Bach, in his *Well-tempered Clavier*, not only imitated the general plan of Fischer's work, but also took over certain fugal themes (cf. *Well-tempered Clavier*, II, fugue in E-major). The suite (No. 248) is taken from Fischer's *Musikalisches Blumenbuschlein*. It is an example of the "ballet suite" of French derivation in which the traditional movements, Allemande, and so on, are discarded. ¶ Sources: (247) J. K. F. Fischer, *Ariadne musica* (Augsburg, 1715); *Sämtliche Werke für Klavier und Orgel von Johann Kaspar Ferdinand Fischer*, edited by E. von Werra (Leipzig, 1901), p. 83. (248) J. K. F. Fischer, *Musikalisches Blumenbüschlein* (Schlagenwerth, 1696); *Sämtliche Werke . . .* (see No. 247), p. 12.

249. JOHANN KRIEGER: "Ricercar" and "Fugue." Krieger is a member of the Middle German school located in Thuringia and the northern part of Bavaria (Nuremberg). The keyboard compositions of this group are characterized by a tendency toward simplicity and modesty in style as well as form. Krieger's ricercar, no doubt one of the latest examples of this old type (see Nos. 115, 116), shows the form's typical traits, that is, slow motion, abstract design, and learned treatment, the last appearing in the consistent use of the inverted theme. Noteworthy is the free contrapuntal texture (*Freistimmigkeit*), which is often encountered in the keyboard fugues of Bach's predecessors (see No. 194). ¶ Sources: J. Krieger, *Anmuthige Clavier-Übung* (Nuremberg, 1698); *DTB*, XVIII, 36, 46.

250, 251. JOHANN PACHELBEL: "Suite ex gis" and "Magnificat Fuga." Pachelbel, the chief representative of the Middle German school (see No. 249), was active in Vienna, Eisenach, and finally as organist of the church of St. Sebald in his native city, Nuremberg. His "Suite ex Gis" (*Gis*, in other words, G-sharp) opens with a passage which is remarkable for its harmonic ventures. The "Magnificat Fugue" is taken from a collection of ninety-four such pieces written for the service at St. Sebald's where, according to the old tradition (see under No. 133), they were played in the place of the even-numbered verses of the Magnificat. They represent the most important source for the study of the organ fugue immediately before Bach. ¶ Sources: (250) *DTB*, II(1), 104. (251) *DTOe*, VIII(2), 58.

252, 253. ARCANGELO CORELLI: "Sonata opus v, no. 3 and no. 8." Corelli, although he worked mostly in Rome, represents the consummation of the Bologna style (see Nos. 219, 245, 246). He brought to fullest realization the tendency of this school toward formal clarity, stylistic elegance, and contrapuntal design. With him the two types of Baroque sonata, the *sonata da chiesa* and the *sonata da camera* (see under No. 245), became definitely established, although deviations from the standard forms still occur. Our *sonata da chiesa*, for instance, has five movements: Adagio, Allegro, Adagio 3/4, Allegro, and Allegro 12/8, the last in the character of a gigue. In a French edition of Corelli's opus v (which includes six sonatas of each type), the slow movements are given in a highly ornamented version, as indicated

at the beginning of our selection. Very likely, Corelli himself used a simpler type of ornamentation (see *BuMBE*, pp. 232ff). ¶ Sources: A. Corelli, *XII Solos for a Violin with a Thorough Bass, op. 5* (London [174?]); *Les Oeuvres de Arcangelo Corelli*, edited by J. Joachim and F. Chrysander (London, 1890), III, 26 (for No. 252), III, 76 (for No. 253); *Class*, no. 9, quad. 29, p. 17 (for No. 252), quad. 32, p. 2 (for No. 253). ¶ Record: (253) *C–69152D*.

254. PHILIPP HEINRICH ERLEBACH: "Himmel, du weisst meine Plagen." Erlebach, who was active in Thuringia, is perhaps the most outstanding German composer of arias in the Baroque period. His *Harmonische Freude* (1679, 1710) is an extensive collection of accompanied songs. It shows his mastery of a great variety of styles and of many types of expression. Our selection is noteworthy for the late-Baroque sweep of its melody as well as for its integrated harmonic structure. ¶ Sources: P. H. Erlebach, *Harmonische Freude Musikalischer Freunde*, vol. II (Nuremberg, 1710); *DdT*, XLVI/XLVII, 216.

255. HENRY PURCELL: "Thy hand, Belinda." Purcell is the one genius who links the greatness of English sixteenth-century music with that of our own time. For many years before him, and certainly for a long time after him, England produced no music of such originality and beauty as his. So original and so bold was Purcell's harmonic idiom that the nineteenth century found it difficult to believe that his music meant what it said. *Dido and Aeneas*, like all of Purcell's music, represents, in its vitality and forthrightness of expression, the best qualities of English musical style. This recitative from *Dido and Aeneas* is an example of the *recitativo arioso* in which a composer, without abandoning the form of the recitative, writes a relatively short solo which approaches the melodic ideal of the aria. The aria "When I am laid in earth" is written over a chromatic ground bass. ¶ Source: *The Works of Henry Purcell*, vol. III, *Dido and Aeneas*, edited by the Purcell Society (London, 1889), p. 84.

256. HENRY PURCELL: "Fantasia." Purcell's fantasias stand at the end of the great tradition of English viol music, forming its artistic consummation. Written at the age of twenty-one (the manuscript carries the inscription: June 10th, 1680), they show a youthful mastery of contrapuntal and harmonic problems which is without parallel in the history of music. In the first movement the treatment of the theme in inversion and in two degrees of augmentation may be noticed. ¶ Sources: London, British Museum, *Add. MS 30930*; *Purcell, Fantasias for Strings*, edited by P. Warlock and A. Mangeot (London, 1927), no. 1. ¶ Record: see *GSE*, p. 361.

257. ANDRÉ CAMPRA: "Cantate Domino." The motet, which up to 1600 was the most important type of sacred music, was sparingly continued during the Baroque period, usually as a composition for solo voices with instrumental accompaniment (see No. 185). Campra, who is known mostly as Lully's successor in the field of opera, published five books

of motets for one to three voices (1695-1720). In our selection the formal elements of the Italian cantata, solo arias, duets, and recitatives, are used for the rendition of a Latin sacred text. ¶ Source: A. Campra, *Motets à 1, 2, 3, voix* . . . (new edition; Paris, 1711), II, 51.

258. ALESSANDRO SCARLATTI: "Mitilde, mio tesor." Alessandro Scarlatti was active mostly in Naples, except for two short periods spent in Rome. He is the central figure of the Neapolitan school which started with Provenzale (see No. 222), but his importance extends much beyond any local limits. Enormously productive, he set new standards in the opera as well as in the cantata and in instrumental ensemble music. More than any other composer, he is the key figure of the late Baroque. Only a small amount of his work has been published, and his cantatas (of which he wrote over six hundred) have been particularly neglected, although it is only in these that "the full range of his musicianship really becomes apparent" (see *BuMBE,* p. 246). A study of our selection, with its truly astonishing flow of expressive melody and inspired harmony, will certainly confirm this opinion. It is in the form of two *da capo* arias, each preceded by a recitative—a form which became standard in Italy. ¶ Source: "Cantate del Sigr. Alessandro Scarlatti" (manuscript copy of *c.* 1800, Boston Public Library, *M. 360.10*), vol. II.

259. ALESSANDRO SCARLATTI: "Sinfonia avanti l'opera." Scarlatti's overture to his opera *La Griselda* (1721) shows the fully developed form of the Italian or Neapolitan overture, as it is called in distinction from the French overture (see Nos. 223, 224). The form is in three short movements, fast-slow-fast, and this form as well as the style is borrowed from the concerto (see Nos. 246, 260). ¶ Source: Brussels, Royal Conservatory, *MS 2352K* (manuscript copy of H. Mishkin).

260. ALESSANDRO SCARLATTI: "Concerto No. 3." Scarlatti is the second great figure in the development of the Baroque concerto, between Torelli (see No. 246) and Vivaldi (see No. 270). The concerto given here clearly foreshadows the much admired dynamism and rhythmic vitality of Vivaldi. The form of this concerto is in five movements, of which the last two, a Largo and an Allegro in gigue style (12/8), have been omitted. ¶ Source: A. Scarlatti, *VI Concertos in Seven Parts* (London [*c.* 1750]), no. 3.

261. JOHANN KUHNAU: "Der todtkranke und wieder gesunde Hiskias." Kuhnau, Bach's predecessor at St. Thomas' in Leipzig, was the first German composer to transfer the instrumental ensemble sonata of the Baroque to the harpsichord. More successful, from the artistic point of view, is his *Musikalische Vorstellungen einiger biblischer Historien* . . . (1700), in which he used the form of the harpsichord sonata for the "Musical Presentations of Sundry Biblical Stories." The present sonata, based on the story of Hezekiah, is number four of these. In the first movement the chorale "Herzlich tut mich verlangen" (indicated by asterisks) is used.

¶ Sources: J. Kuhnau, *Musikalische Vorstellung einiger biblischen Historien* (Leipzig, 1700); *DdT,* IV, 158.

262. GIOVANNI BATTISTA BONONCINI: "Deh lascia, o core." Bononcini, born in Modena, was active in Vienna, Rome, and Berlin before he went to London in 1717, where he became the adversary of Handel in a rivalry which took on a distinctly political character, the Hanoverian king taking Handel's side, the nobility siding with Bononcini. His compositions show a great lyrical talent and, although not very profound, often have an irresistible charm. Ambros characterized them as having "a perfect, though somewhat vacant beauty." *Astianatte,* from which opera our aria is taken, was composed in 1727. ¶ Source: F. A. Gevaert, *Les Gloires d'Italie,* II (Paris, 1888), 131.

263. TOMMASO ANTONIO VITALI: "Sonata No. 4." Tommaso Vitali is the last member of the Bologna school. Our sonata shows the characteristic traits of the fully developed Baroque trio sonata, such as the running bass in the first Adagio, and the imitative treatment of all the three strings in the two Allegros. ¶ Source: T. A. Vitali, *Sonate a tre per doi violini e violoncello con basso per l'organo,* op. 1 (Modena, 1693; manuscript copy of H. Mishkin).

264. JOHN CHRISTOPHER PEPUSCH: "My love is all madness" and "Hither, dear husband." The ballad opera represented in part, at least, a reaction against the tyranny exercised by Italian opera in England. Of works of this type, *The Beggar's Opera* (1728) is the best known. The text was written by John Gay and the music arranged by J. C. Pepusch, a German by birth but long resident in England. As their name implies, the musical material of ballad operas was drawn largely from the melodies of ballads, the popular character of which may be observed in our illustrations (see *GrSHO,* pp. 259ff). ¶ Sources: *The Beggar's Opera, Written by Mr. Gay* (3d edition; London, 1729), act III, scene i, act III, scene xii, Appendix, "The Songs," pp. 31, 38; *Twelve Famous Plays of the Restoration and Eighteenth Century* (Modern Library edition; New York, 1933), pp. 641 (air 2), 644 (air 12).

265. FRANÇOIS COUPERIN: "Le Rossignol en amour" and "Sœur Monique." Couperin the Great, as he was called in order to distinguish him from the numerous other musicians in his family (see No. 229), was organist at St. Gervais in Paris and court clavecinist to Louis XIV. Although older than Bach by almost twenty years, he was the first representative of a new period of music history, the Rococo. The change of style from Baroque seriousness and profundity to Rococo charm and elegance is particularly apparent in his numerous compositions for the harpsichord, which he published in four books of *Pièces de clavecin* between 1713 and 1730. "Sœur Monique" is one of his numerous pieces cast in the form of the rondeau. ¶ Sources: F. Couperin, *Le Troisième livre de pièces de clavecin* (Paris, 1722); *Pièces de clavecin composées par François Couperin,* edited by J.

Brahms and F. Chrysander (London, 1871ff), III, 241, 301; *Early Keyboard Music,* edited by L. Oesterle (New York, 1904), II, 18.

266. FRANÇOIS COUPERIN: "Qui dat nivem." Although mostly known for his harpsichord pieces, Couperin was also active, though more conservatively, in the field of vocal music. With works like the present selection he continued the activity of earlier French composers of motets, like Charpentier (see No. 226) and Campra (see No. 257). The extremely high range of this composition, together with the choice of two flutes for the accompaniment, produces an unusual tonal quality which must have had a special attraction for the French audience of that day. In the original score the "bassus continuus" is notated in unison with the violins, an octave higher than in our score. No doubt, it was played with a sixteen-foot stop which caused it to sound an octave below the violins. If notated as in the original there is hardly room for the thorough-bass accompaniment. In this piece the note values found in the source have been brought into conformity with modern practice, and grace notes indicating long appogiaturas have been rendered in notes of normal size. ¶ Sources: F. Couperin, *Quatre versets d'un motet . . .* (Paris, 1705); *Oeuvres complètes de François Couperin,* edited by M. Cauchie, XI (Paris, 1932), 109.

267. REINHARD KEISER: "Fahret wohl." Throughout the earlier part of the seventeenth century opera flourished in Germany only sporadically at courtly residences such as Vienna, Dresden, and Munich where works of Italian or, later, French composers were performed for special occasions (see, for instance, No. 221). The first native operatic composer of importance was Keiser, who was active in Hamburg, where later Handel became his rival and Telemann (see No. 271) his successor. Fully deserving of the praise given to him by men like Steffani and Handel, Keiser appears as an operatic talent of the first order. His sureness of style and fertility of invention have been compared to those of Mozart (*GrSHO,* p. 158). Our selection from the early opera *Adonis* (1697) is remarkable not only for lyrical and expressive vocal lines, but also for its instrumental part in which the then current idiom of a "running bass" is imaginatively used. ¶ Source: *Adonis* (1697; manuscript copy of H. Leichtentritt), act II, scene i.

268. WILLIAM CROFT: "Put me not to rebuke." The word "verse" at the beginning of the second movement indicates the use of solo voices; and this anthem, therefore, although it lacks the variety characteristic of the earlier verse anthems, conforms to type at least to the extent of including a number of separate movements, and in its use of solo voices. In the skill displayed in writing for the chorus as well as in its contrapuntal method it looks back to the seventeenth century rather than forward to the style which later characterized the typical eighteenth-century English anthem (see No. 279). The final choral section of this example has been omitted. ¶ Sources: W. Boyce, *Cathedral Music* (see No. 242), II, 193; J. Warren, *Cathedral Music . . .* (see No. 242), III, 81.

269. EVARISTO FELICE DALL' ABACO: "Sonata opus III, no. 2." Abaco was an Italian who worked mainly at the court of Munich, where he was greatly honored. His works stand in succession to those of Corelli, which they often surpass in expressive power and inner logic. Our selection is the second of four movements: Adagio-Allegro-Largo-Allegro. ¶ Sources: E. F. dall' Abaco, *XII Sonate da chiesa e da camera,* op. 3 (Paris [1715?]); *DTB,* I, 89. ¶ Record: *AS-46.*

270. ANTONIO VIVALDI: "Concerto opus III, no. 6." Vivaldi was born in Venice where he held the position of director of the *Ospedale della Pietà* from 1713 until his death. He brought the Italian concerto to an admirable peak of perfection, clarifying its formal structure and imbuing it with a characteristic breathless drive and uniform continuity (see *BuMBE,* p. 230). Bach transcribed several of Vivaldi's concertos for the harpsichord, among them the one reproduced here. This is a concerto grosso with a concertino of three violins; it is in three movements: fast-slow-fast. It is the sixth of his *Estro harmonico* (Harmonical Whim). ¶ Source: A. Vivaldi, *L'Estro harmonico,* op. 3 (Amsterdam [1715?]), no. 6. ¶ Record: *D-20105/6.*

271, 272. GEORG PHILIPP TELEMANN: "Sonata" and "Chor der Seligen." Telemann was not only the most prolific but also one of the most successful and most prosperous composers of the eighteenth century. He was equally at ease in the various national styles of the period, and many of his several thousands of compositions show a most attractive combination of good workmanship, artistic ingenuity, and pleasant refinement which made them much more popular in his day than the works of Bach. Our selection No. 271 is the first movement of a sonata (Soave-Allegro-Andante-Vivace) which is among the earlier works of Telemann. In his later compositions, such as the oratorio *Der Tag des Gerichts* (The Day of Judgment) of 1761 and the monodrama *Ino* of 1765, there are many instances of a true dramatic expression which indicates the change from the gallant style to that of "storm and stress." The accompaniment in No. 271 is a realization of the figured bass, and the notation should be identical with that used in the other realizations. Our chorus (No. 272) from *Der Tag des Gerichts* represents, no doubt, a lofty vision of apocalyptic greatness. ¶ Sources: (271) G. P. Telemann, *Six quatuors à violon, flute, viole ou violoncelle et basse continue* (c. 1735; manuscript copy of J. M. Oldenburg). (272) *DdT,* XXVIII, 101.

273. FRANCESCO DURANTE: "Fiero acerbo." Durante, although he was born and lived in Naples, remained aloof from the opera, and worked mostly in the fields of church music and the chamber cantata. In this respect as well as in his cultivation of a serious, contrapuntal style he seems closer to the Roman than to the Neapolitan school. His twelve "Duetti da camera" are remarkable for their daring exploitation of chromatic melodies and harmonies, although one can-

not help feeling that the boldness of his imagination is not as great as is the boldness of his idiom. ¶ Sources: "Cantate del Sigr. Durante" (manuscript copy of *c.* 1800, Boston Public Library, *M. 360.3*); *Duetti del Sigr. Durante,* revised and corrected by Cherubini (Paris [182?]), p. 43; *XII Duetti da camera composte da Francesco Durante* (Leipzig [184?]), II, 16.

274. DOMENICO SCARLATTI: "Sonata." Domenico, the son of Alessandro Scarlatti, was born in Naples and was active in Rome, London, Lisbon, and Madrid. His devotion to the harpsichord was as absolute as was Chopin's devotion to the pianoforte. His more than three hundred "sonatas," as his one-movement pieces are usually called, represent a contribution to the development of keyboard music comparable to that of the English virginalists (see Nos. 177–179) and of Chopin and Liszt. Fascinating because of their unemotional detachment, clear precision, and technical brilliance, Scarlatti's sonatas often show a mosaic-like succession of various repeated patterns which give the pieces a somewhat static quality, in spite of all the fast motion which usually prevails from the beginning to the end. Our selection is of special interest owing to the extensive use of dissonant *acciacaturas.* ¶ Source: *Domenico Scarlatti, opere complete per clavicembalo,* edited by A. Longo (Milan, 1913), no. 429. ¶ Record: *MC-1091.*

275. GIUSEPPE TARTINI: "Sonata opus III, no. 12." Tartini, born in Pirano (Istria), worked from 1721 until his death in Padua where he became the founder of an important school of violin playing, often called the "School of Nations." As a composer he continued the trend toward the *goût galant* in violin music which had been inaugurated by Veracini (1685?–1750) and Geminiani (1674?–1762?). Both of these men, however, he surpassed through the variety of his musical imagination, which shows dramatic and expressive as well as romantic and humorous facets. Our example, the last movement of a sonata Andante-Allegro-Presto assai, clearly foreshadows the gaiety of a Haydn finale. ¶ Source: G. Tartini, *XII Sonate a violino e basso,* op. 3 (Paris [*c.* 1750]), no. 12.

276, 277. JEAN PHILIPPE RAMEAU: "Ramage des oiseaux" and "Sommeil." "The French opera entered its most glorious phase with Rameau, whose operas represent one of the highest achievements of French music" (*BuMBE,* p. 254). Rameau's operas are indeed a mine of musical treasures which still remain to be fully recognized and explored. The "Ramage des oiseaux" (The Warbling of the Birds) is the final scene from *Le Temple da la Gloire* (1745; text by Voltaire), in which the hero, Trajan, finds himself at the peak of his glory, and, listening to the birds, beholds a happy country and people. The rondeau "Sommeil" (Slumber) from *Dardanus* (1739) is instrumental music accompanying a dream scene. ¶ Sources: (276) J. P. Rameau, *Le Temple de la Gloire* (Paris, 1745), act III, scene v; *Rameau, oeuvres complètes,* publiée sous la direction de C. Saint-

Saëns, XIV (Paris, 1909), 333. (277) J. P. Rameau, *Dardanus* (Paris, 1739), act IV, scene i; Saint-Saëns edition (see No. 276), x (Paris, 1905), 310.

278. JEAN MARIE LECLAIR: "Sonata opus V, no. 12." Leclair was the most outstanding representative of the French violin school of the eighteenth century. He remained closer to the Baroque tradition than, for instance, Tartini (see No. 275), a fact which is demonstrated by stylistic considerations as well as by his customary employment of the four-movement scheme of the *sonata da chiesa.* Our sonata consists of Adagio, Allegro, Largo, and Ciaccona. The abundant but always meaningful ornamentations of the movement reproduced here illustrate the French style of violin playing which was also applied in France to the sonatas of Corelli (see No. 252; cf. *BuMBE,* pp. 250f). One notational feature preserved from the source of this selection is the rendering of all note values shorter than the sixteenth note as thirty-second notes. ¶ Source: J. M. Leclair, *Troisième livre de sonates à violon seul . . .* op. v (Paris [1738?]).

279. MAURICE GREENE: "Acquaint thyself with God." Greene is generally viewed as one of the foremost English church composers of the eighteenth century. In the florid style of both solo voice and organ, this multi-sectional, cantata-type of anthem is much more characteristic of the period than is No. 268, although the lifetimes of Croft and Greene overlap. Particularly reminiscent of Handel, though characteristic of other eighteenth-century composers as well, is the restatement of the first phrase after a brief instrumental interlude—Handel strongly influenced English musical art, and Greene is said to have greatly admired Handel's music—but aside from this device of restatement there is little if anything in this selection that indicates more than an awareness of Handel's style. A section for bass and a concluding choral section are omitted. ¶ Sources: M. Greene, *Cathedral Music* (London [*c.* 1760]), I, 15; *The Forty Select Anthems by Dr. Maurice Greene,* edited by V. Novello (London [184?]), I, 17; *Cathedral Anthems,* no. C5, a new series edited by C. H. Stewart (London, 1925).

280. THEOPHIL (GOTTLIEB) MUFFAT: "Final." The German Rococo found a happy realization in the harpsichord music of Georg Muffat's son, Theophil, who was court organist at Vienna. His suites, like those of Handel, usually combine dance movements with abstract sonata movements, such as the "Final" reproduced here. This is an example of the "rounded binary form" from which the sonata form of the classical period derives (see *HDM,* s.v. "Binary and ternary form, II"). The exact meaning of the three R's in the second part is not clear. Probably the final thirteen measures are to be repeated, as a ritornello. ¶ Sources: T. Muffat, *Componimenti musicali per il cembalo* (Augsburg [*c.* 1735]); *DTOe,* III(3), 20.

281. JOHANN ADOLF HASSE: "Ma giunge appunto." Hasse, who was born near Hamburg in 1699, went to Naples in 1722. Completely Italianized, he became a leading repre-

sentative of the Neapolitan school (see *GrSHO*, pp. 210f). His oratorio, *La conversione di Sant' Agostino*, was first given in 1750. Our selection is taken from the beginning of the oratorio, where Augustine's father and mother anxiously await the return of their son. It is an example of the *recitativo accompagnato* which, unlike the *recitativo secco* (see No. 206), employs the orchestra as accompaniment. Thus the orchestra assumes a partnership with the singer, at times emphasizing the text by instrumental commentary. ¶ Sources: Autograph (?) *MS* of 1752 in the Boston Public Library; *DdT*, xx, 8.

282. KARL HEINRICH GRAUN: "Godi l'amabile." Graun was in the employ of Frederick the Great who, in 1740, entrusted him with the establishment of opera in Berlin. *Montezuma* belongs to the year 1755, and the libretto for it was written by the king. The work was composed near the end of Graun's life and shows the experience gained from the composition of over a score of earlier operatic works. In Graun's time Italian style and the Italian language dominated the opera in Germany. The aria here included is German in spirit even to the point of suggesting in some particulars the method of Gluck; but the presence of Italian style is self-evident. ¶ Source: *DdT*, xv, 36.

283. GIOVANNI BATTISTA SAMMARTINI: "Symphony in D-major." Sammartini, who was organist at Milan, was one of the earliest composers to write symphonies, that is, independent orchestral compositions modeled after the operatic sinfonias of Alessandro Scarlatti (see No. 259) and his successors. Our example, taken from a three-movement symphony composed in 1740, seems to be quite Handelian in character but upon closer examination reveals traits foreshadowing the dynamic style of the Mannheimers (see No. 294), particularly in the two bold unison passages near the end. ¶ Source: *Sammlung Sondheimer* (Basle, 1937), no. 49 (numerous editorial marks have been omitted).

284. GIOVANNI PLATTI: "Sonata opus 1, no. 2." Platti, about whom little is known, except that he worked in Bamberg and Würzberg from 1724 to 1749, was one of the first composers to write sonatas in the style of the Italian Rococo, a style that found its highest development in Mozart. In the six sonatas of his opus 1, Platti still adheres to the four-movement scheme, slow-fast-slow-fast, of the *sonata da chiesa*. The single movements, however, particularly the fast ones, are written in a novel idiom obviously influenced by Pergolesi's *opera buffa* style (see Nos. 286, 287). Very likely Platti was expressly referring to Pergolesi in the words "sur le goût italien" found in the title of his opus 1, a publication which probably appeared about 1742, six years after Pergolesi's premature death. The selection used here is the last movement of a sonata consisting of Adagio-Allegro-Larghetto-Allegro. ¶ Source: G. Platti, *VI Sonates pour le clavessin sur le goût italien*, op. 1 (Nuremberg [*c.* 1742]), p. 37.

285. BALDASSARE GALUPPI: "Da me non speri." Galuppi spent his life in Venice, except for two periods of

activity in Petersburg (now Leningrad), then the capital of Russia. He is mainly known today as the composer of somewhat trifling harpsichord sonatas, but in his time he was famous as an operatic composer, particularly in the field of the comic opera where he successfully continued along the lines inaugurated by his younger contemporary, Pergolesi (see Nos. 286, 287). *Il filosofo di campagna* was produced in 1754. ¶ Sources: B. Galuppi, *Il filosofo di campagna* (1750; manuscript copy in the Boston Public Library); *Class*, no. 13, quad. 58, p. 22.

286, 287. GIOVANNI BATTISTA PERGOLESI: "Le virtuose" and "Lo conosco." Pergolesi's fame as a composer of comic opera (*opera buffa*) is well known. Although his *La serva padrona* (1733) was by no means the first comic intermezzo (that is, a short and lively play designed to be performed between the acts of a serious opera; see *GrSHO*, p. 248), it surpasses the earlier as well as the later ones in its power of characterization and in its natural charm. While *La serva padrona* deals with the successful intrigues by which a girl rises from the status of servant to that of mistress of an old and wealthy bachelor, *Il maestro di musica* centers around the well-known figure of a vain and overbearing singing teacher. Collagiani's aria is remarkable for its many amusing details; for instance, the musical characterization of the "fermate, fulminate, trilli, cadenze, arcisaltate" and the subtly ironic misaccentuation at the end ("árcisáltaté," "pótutó"). ¶ Sources: (286) G. B. Pergolesi, *Le Maistre de musique* (Paris, 1752), act ii, scene i; *Opera omnia di G. B. Pergolesi,* edited by F. Caffarelli (Rome, 1940–1942), xxv, 28. (287) G. B. Pergolesi, *La Servante maîtresse* (Paris [after 1754]), p. 30; G. B. Pergolesi, *La serva padrona* (Milan, 1908), p. 19; *Opera omnia* (see No. 286), xi, 24; *Class,* no. 23, quad. 89–90, p. 22.

288, 289. WILHELM FRIEDEMANN BACH: "Polonaise" and "Fugue." Wilhelm Friedemann, the eldest son of J. S. Bach, has suffered considerably from misrepresentation by some of his earlier biographers. In the estimation of many musicians, however, he was the most gifted of Bach's sons. The pre-Romantic period of "sensitivity" and "storm and stress" found in him a most eloquent representative, perhaps the only one who was able to elevate its somewhat formalistic methods to a truly expressive musical language. In their dynamic intensity and boldness, many of his compositions come surprisingly close to Beethoven. ¶ Sources: (288) Manuscript copy in the collection of G. B. Weston, Cambridge, Massachusetts; J. H. Farrenc, *Le Trésor des pianistes,* vi (Paris, 1865), 4; *Fugen und Polonaisen . . . von Wilh. Friedemann Bach,* edited by W. Niemann (Leipzig, 1914), p. 28. (289) *Le Trésor des pianistes* (see No. 288), ix, 41; *Fugen und Polonaisen* (see No. 288), p. 11.

290. THOMAS AUGUSTINE ARNE: "Come, O come." This song is an example of pure eighteenth-century English lyricism at its best. Arne undoubtedly admired Italian style, but the Italianate music he wrote is far from convincing and is, in quality, quite inferior to the products of his own

native English feeling. The example given here is taken from *The Fall of Phaeton* (1736). ¶Source: *Six Songs by Thomas Augustine Arne,* edited by G. E. P. Arkwright, The Old English Edition, II (London, 1890), 21.

291. JEAN JACQUES ROUSSEAU: "Allons danser." Rousseau, the famous philosopher, holds a position in the history of music not only as the author of a famous *Dictionnaire* (1767) and other writings on music, but also as an operatic composer. His *Devin du village* (The Village Soothsayer; 1752) marks the beginnings of the French comic opera (see No. 306). Composed during the famous "War of the Buffoons," which split Paris into an "Italian" and a "French" party, it may be said to represent the peace treaty between the warring groups. Rousseau adopted the Italian form with continuous music and recitatives, in contrast to the earlier *vaudeville* comedies which had only interspersed music, but retained nonetheless the natural simplicity and popular character of the *vaudevilles* (see *GrSHO*, p. 256). ¶Source: J. Rousseau, *Le Devin du village* (Paris, 1752), scene viii. ¶Record: *AS–54.*

292, 293. CHRISTOPH WILLIBALD GLUCK: "Chiamo il mio ben" and "Diane impitoyable." *Orfeo* (1762) is the first realization of Gluck's attempt to do away with the conventions and artificialities of Italian opera. A comparison of this selection with an aria from one of Gluck's earlier works such as *Le nozze d'Ercole e d'Ebe* (1747) will show his preference for the more classical type of operatic melody. It is in *Alceste* (1767), however, with its preface setting forth Gluck's conviction regarding what an opera should be, in melody as in all other things, that Gluck's importance in the history of opera becomes manifest. Five years after *Alceste* came *Iphegeneia in Aulis.* "Diane impitoyable," drawn from that opera, displays Gluck at the height of his powers as melodist, dramatist, and musician. Among the many features of this excerpt, which confirm Gluck's views as expounded in the *Alceste* preface, none is more significant than the appearance of recitative in the midst of the aria rather than at the beginning, a position which it held in the Italian-style opera of the day. ¶Sources: (292) C. W. Gluck, *Orfeo ed Euridice* (Paris, 1762), act I, scene ii; *DTOe,* xxI(2), 36. (293) C. W. Gluck, *Iphigénie en Aulide* (Paris, 1774); act I, scene i; *Iphigenia in Aulis by C. von Gluck,* revised edition by B. Tours (London, 1927).

294. JOHANN STAMITZ: "Symphony opus v, no. 2." Although former claims for Johann Stamitz as "the" founder of the symphony have proved exaggerated, nevertheless he stands out as the boldest among the early symphonists. He was the founder of the Mannheim school, so called after the location of the orchestra which he conducted and which he made famous for its novel style of playing. Our example, the first of four movements (Presto-Andantino-Menuetto-Prestissimo), clearly shows his revolutionary and uncompromising approach, his exploitation of dynamic contrasts, his extended crescendos over a passage in determined upward motion, and his fondness for violin tremolos, hardly used

since Monteverdi (see No. 189). ¶Source: *DTB,* vII(2), 55 (some of the additions and variants found in the oboe part of the early printed edition have been incorporated in our reproduction, in square brackets).

295. GEORG MATTHIAS MONN: "Symphony in D-major." Monn is the Viennese counterpart of Stamitz. His symphonies, pre-Haydn and Mozart rather than pre-Beethoven, lack the militant drive of the Mannheim master, but are remarkable for their inner balance and formal clarity. Our symphony, which is dated "24. Mai 1740," has four movements, Allegro-Aria-Menuetto-Allegro, and has been called "the first complete symphony" (P. Lang, *Music in Western Civilization,* 1941, p. 607). The last movement, reproduced here, is a short but complete example of sonata form. ¶Source: *DTOe,* xv(2), 47.

296, 297. KARL PHILIPP EMANUEL BACH: "Fantasia" and "Sonata." Although perhaps less brilliantly gifted than his elder brother Friedemann, Karl Philipp Emanuel achieved important results through his seriousness of purpose and his penetration into the problems of the period. His compositions are not free from a mannered quality and from an exaggeration of expression, which are the results of intellectual reflection rather than of creative spontaneity. Nevertheless, there is much to be admired in the works of a man whom Haydn and Beethoven revered as their "musical father." ¶Sources: (296) K. P. E. Bach, *Musikalisches Vielerley* (Hamburg, 1770), p. 13. (297) K. P. E. Bach, *Sechs Klaviersonaten für Kenner und Liebhaber,* Erste Sammlung (Leipzig, 1779), no. 3; *Klavierwerke von Carl Philipp Emanuel Bach,* edited by C. Krebs, Urtext Klassischer Musikwerke (Leipzig, 1895), p. 16; *Klavierwerke von Philipp Emanuel Bach,* edited by H. Schenker (Vienna, 1902), p. 86.

298. DOMENICO TERRADELLAS: "In vasto mare infido." Terradellas was a Spaniard who as a youth went to Naples to study. Later he was active mainly in Rome where Jommelli (see No. 299) was his most successful rival in the operatic field. Both of them also composed for the church, transferring the operatic style to the motet. ¶Source: Brussels, Royal Conservatory, *MS F.G.33.885.*

299. NICCOLÒ JOMMELLI: "Mors et vita." Jommelli, born in Naples, was active in that city as well as in Rome, Bologna, Venice, and Stuttgart where he became familiar with the novel methods of the Mannheim school. Our selection is taken from his composition of the Easter sequence, "Victimae paschali laudes" (see No. 16b). The highly virtuoso style of writing indicates the possibility that this was written not for a chorus, but for four soloists. To have included all the relatively unimportant differences, which occur in measures 26 and 27, between the first statement and the repeat would have resulted in a confused looking score. The selection of a whole note as the final note in our version is arbitrary; at this point in the source the music merges into another movement. ¶Source: N. Jommelli, *Sequentia pas-*

*chalis a sei voci* (manuscript copy in the Boston Public Library, *M.120.22*).

**300. NICOLA PICCINNI:** "Achetez à ma boutique." Piccinni studied in Naples and was active in Rome and later in Paris where he was the main rival of Gluck (quarrel of the Gluckists and Piccinnists; see *GrSHO*, pp. 241f). Our selection from *Le Faux Lord,* in which the hero, Le Fleur, approaches Irene in the disguise of a peddler, shows Piccinni's gift for characterization in comic scenes. ¶ Source: N. Piccinni, *Le Faux Lord* (Paris [177?]), act I, scene iv.

**301. JOHANN ADAM HILLER:** "Bald die Blonde, bald die Braune." Hiller worked in Leipzig, where he became the first conductor of the famous *Gewandhaus* concerts (1781). He is the outstanding representative of the German *Singspiel,* which owed its rise chiefly to the influx of the English ballad opera (see No. 264; cf. *GrSHO*, pp. 263ff). The *Singspiel* was an amateur opera in the character of a spoken comedy with interspersed songs, either sentimental or jolly, and always in simple folk style. Our selection from *Lisuart und Dariolette* (1766) is a song of Lisuart's servant Derwin, who expresses his dissatisfaction with his position and with the amorous whims of his master in a manner strikingly similar to that of Leporello in the famous "Catalogue Aria" from Mozart's *Don Giovanni.* ¶ Source: J. A. Hiller, *Lisuart und Dariolette* (Leipzig, 1769), act IV.

**302. GIOVANNI MARIA PLACIDO RUTINI:** "Sonata opus VI, no. 6." This example has been selected to represent the Italian branch of the pre-Classical sonata. Completely under the influence of the gallant Rococo style, composers like Rutini, Galuppi, Pescetti, Paganelli, and many others wrote numerous sonatas, some of which have often been reprinted. Although on the whole somewhat trifling and facile, they contain much of the material which Mozart was to use with consummate artistry. Our selection is the last of three movements, Andante-Presto assai-Allegro. ¶Source: G. M. P. Rutini, *Sei sonate per cimbalo,* op. VI (Nuremberg [c. 1760]; manuscript copy of A. Einstein).

**303. JOHANN CHRISTIAN BACH:** "Sonata opus XVII, no. 4." J. S. Bach's youngest son, Johann Christian, was active in Milan (where he embraced Catholicism) and in London. His stay in Italy brought him into contact with the Rococo style of Rutini and others (see No. 302), to whose somewhat superficial elegance he added a healthy admixture of German directness and seriousness. In this happy amalgamation he, more than anyone else, appears as the musical father of Mozart. The first movement reproduced here is a fully developed example of sonata form of the type often found in Mozart and Haydn, that is, with the initial theme stated at the beginning of the development section (see remark under No. 308). This last remnant of the original binary form disappeared gradually in the later works of these masters. ¶Sources: J. C. Bach, *Six Sonatas for the Harpsichord or Piano Forte,* op. XVII (London [177?]); *Zehn Klavierso-*

*naten von Joh. Christian Bach,* edited by L. Landshoff (Leipzig, 1925), p. 35.

**304. JOHANN FRIEDRICH EDELMANN:** "Sonata opus 1, no. 1." Edelmann, Schobert, Eckardt, Hüllmandel, and other composers of German descent form an interesting but little-known school of Parisian pre-Classicism. They cultivated particularly the then novel pianoforte, usually in combination with a violin which served as an accompaniment for the pianoforte (*sic*) and which, indeed, often merely doubled the upper piano part. Stylistically, these sonatas derive from the pre-Classicism of Mannheim and Vienna (see Nos. 294, 295). Our sonata is in three movements, Allegro-Polonaise-Allegro molto. ¶Source: J. F. Edelmann, *Six Grand Lessons for the Forte Piano or Harpsichord with an Accompaniment for a Violin . . .* op. 1 (London [c. 1780]).

**305. KARL DITTERS VON DITTERSDORF:** "Schlaflied des Sturmwald." Karl Ditters (von Dittersdorf after a title of nobility) was a native of Vienna who served as a music master to several princes in Austria, Hungary, and Bohemia. He is a representative of the Viennese *Singspiel,* as Hiller is of the North German type of *Singspiel* (see No. 301). His comic operas are much more extended and developed than those of Hiller. They show a mixture of Viennese humor and Italian bravura which found a more exquisite expression in Mozart. Sturmwald, an invalid captain, is the elderly rival for the hand of the daughter of the apothecary, who is in love with the son of the doctor. In our scene Sturmwald makes ready to guard her against being abducted by her lover, but immediately falls asleep. ¶ Sources: K. D. von Dittersdorf, *Doctor und Apotheker* (1786), act I; new edition by R. Kleinmichel (Leipzig [1890]), p. 106.

**306. ANDRÉ ERNEST MODESTE GRÉTRY:** "Et zic et zic." Grétry, a prolific composer of French comic operas, is best remembered for his *Richard Coeur-de-Lion* (1784). This work is noteworthy not only as an early example of the "rescue" opera cultivated so much by later composers (Mozart's *Abduction;* Beethoven's *Fidelio;* Meyerbeer's *Robert le Diable*), but also for its romantic qualities, its extended use of a leitmotiv (see the article in *HDM*), and, in general, the natural charm of its music. Completely unconcerned with the finer details of harmony, counterpoint, or orchestration, Grétry gave his undivided attention to pleasing melody and careful treatment of the text. Our selection shows a characteristically French idiom which has survived to the present day among the street singers of France. Differences between the first statement and the repetition are indicated by small notes with the figure 2. ¶ Sources: A. E. M. Grétry, *Richard Coeur-de-Lion* (Paris, 1784), act III, scene ix; *Collection complète des oeuvres de Grétry,* publiée par le gouvernement Belge (Leipzig [1883–1936]), I, 205.

**307. LUIGI BOCCHERINI:** "Minuetto." The string quartet, which emerged about 1750 (see the article in *HDM*), found an eloquent and prolific champion in Haydn's contemporary, Boccherini, who seems to have grasped the importance of this new medium before Haydn became interested in it. Their respective attitudes toward this genre are neatly described by the saying that "Boccherini is the wife of Haydn." ¶ Sources: L. Boccherini, *Sei quartetti concertanti per due violini, alto e violoncello,* op. 27 (Paris [*c.* 1778]); *Boccherini, sei quartetti per archi,* edited by E. Polo (Milan, 1928), second series, p. 50.

308. MANUEL BLASCO DE NEBRA: "Sonata opus 1, no. 5." This Spanish composer was entirely unknown until recently, when a sonata of his was published by William S. Newman in *Thirteen Keyboard Sonatas of the 18th and 19th Centuries* (Chapel Hill, 1947). The influence of Domenico Scarlatti can be noticed in many details, such as the repetition of short patterns, the extended range of broken-chord figures, and the wide skips involving crossing of hands. Each of the six sonatas of his opus 1, the only work through which he is known to us, consists of two extended movements, the first suggestive of slow tempo, the second of fast. The fast movements often show a certain dramatic impetuosity. This selection is a fairly well-developed example of sonata form, with two distinct thematic groups, and with a development section that avoids starting out with the first theme (see Nos. 284, 295, 303, 304). This indicates an important step in the transformation leading from the rounded binary form to the sonata form. ¶ Source: M. B. de Nebra, *Seis sonatas para clave, y fuerte piano,* op. 1 (Seville [*c.* 1780]).

309. SAMUEL WEBBE: "Glorious Apollo" and "Hot Cross Buns." The first glee club was organized in London in the latter part of the eighteenth century. In 1790 Webbe composed the glee "Glorious Apollo," and thereafter this piece was invariably sung to open the meetings of the club. The glee is generally for three voices, harmonically written, unaccompanied, in the major or minor mode, periodically constructed, and composed on subjects as varied as those of the earlier madrigals. Our second selection is a catch. This genre, which dates from the late sixteenth century, was at first identical with the round; but at a later stage in its development the texts were often arranged so as to bring the words of the different parts into comic juxtaposition. ¶ Sources: (a) *The Harmonist,* 1 (London [179?]), 4; *Boosey and Company's National Edition of Standard English Glees,* 1 (London, 1866), 248. (b) *An Eighth Book of Glees, Canons and Catches* (London [179?]), p. 27.

310. FRANCIS HOPKINSON: "Beneath a weeping willow's shade." Our anthology closes with a composition indicating the appearance of American composers on the musical scene. Hopkinson, famous as a statesman and signer of the Declaration of Independence, was a man of high culture and broad interests. According to known records, he is the first native-born American composer. His songs are written in the then current style of English sentimental lyrics (Arnold, Shield, Storace, and others). ¶ Sources: F. Hopkinson, *Seven Songs for the Harpsichord or Forte Piano* (Philadelphia, 1788), p. 3; *Six Songs by Francis Hopkinson,* edited and augmented by H. V. Milligan (Boston, 1918), p. 12.

# TRANSLATIONS

182.                    *Funeste piaggi*

*Venus:* Pray, sigh and weep, perhaps it will come to pass that that soft lament which moved Heaven may cause Hell yet to submit.

*Orpheus:* Sad shores, shadowy, horrid fields,
That never saw twinkling stars or light of sun,
Resound grieving
To the sound of my anguished words,
While with sad accents
I sigh for my lost happiness with you.
And you, alas, through pity for my martyrdom
Which remains eternal in my wretched heart,
Weep at my lament, shades of Hades.
Alas, alas! At dawn the sun of my eyes has reached its
    setting.
Wretch, wretch! and at that hour
That I thought to warm myself in its fair rays,
Death put out the beautiful light; and cold and alone
    did I remain betwixt lament and grief
As a serpent is wont on a cold hillside in winter.
Weep at my lament, shades of Hades.

183.                    *A questi suoni*

*Body:* At these sounds and songs
I feel my soul moving
Like the leaf in the wind.

*Soul:* How dost thou quickly change!
Be strong and have no fear.
This is false pleasure.

*Pleasure and Companions:*

(1) Songs, laughter, and beguiling love,
Cool waters, soft meadows, gentle breezes,
Pleasing harmonies that cheer the heart,
Banquets, sweetmeats, and delicious feasts;

(2) Beautiful raiment and fragrant perfumes,
Pageants and festivities full of joy,
Pleasure, delight, and jubilation:
Happy the soul that can enjoy them.

*Soul:* I do not believe you, no, no;
I know you are deceptions;
All your offerings which seem entrancing
Are, in the end, all bitter.
Happy the soul that can resist them.

184.                    *Sfogava con le stelle*

He gave vent with the stars
To an inferno of love
Under the night sky [he gave vent] to his grief
And he said, gazing upon them:
Oh, oh, images of my idol whom I adore,
Just as you show to me
While thus you shine,

Her rare beauty,
So did you show to her
As you shine
My burning ardors.
Would that you would make her with your golden appearance
As full of pity, as you make me a lover.

185.                    *Exaudi me, Domine*

Hear me, O Lord; for thy loving kindness is good: turn unto me according to the multitude of thy tender mercies.

And hide not thy face from thy servant; for I am in trouble: hear me speedily.            Psalm 69:16, 17

186.                    *Il zapaione musicale*

Since we are few in number let us sing joyfully. Who will be soprano? I will, who have it in hand. Will this be the alto? Here I stand forth. Here is the tenor. You, for our love. Who will sing treble? If I sing it I will have delight. There remains the bass. I will sing it for pleasure. Now we are agreed let us taste for pleasure this nice eggnog.

187.                    *Ma che temi*

*Orpheus:* But what are you afraid of, my heart? That which Pluto forbids love commands.
    I should certainly obey the more powerful divinity who conquers both men and gods.
    (*Here a noise occurs behind the curtain . . . Orpheus continues singing to the harpsichord, violin, and guitar.*)
    But what do I hear? Alas, miserable me. Perhaps the Furies in love are with rage taking up arms to hurt me and to snatch from me my happiness, and I consent to it?
    (*Here Orpheus turns and sings to the accompaniment of the wooden organ.*)
    Oh sweetest lights, I can even see you, I can . . .
    (*Here Orpheus sings to the tune of the harpsichord, violin, and guitar.*)
    But what eclipse, alas, is darkening you?

*A Spirit:* You have broken the law and you are unworthy of pardon.

*Eurydice:* Ah sight that is both too sweet and too bitter. Thus you lose me because of too great love? And I, miserable, lose the power of enjoying further light and vision, and I lose you at the same time, the dearest of all my happiness, oh my husband.

*Orpheus:* Where do you go, my life? I follow you. But who denies it to me, alas? Wild dream, what hidden power of these horrors drags me, against my will, away from these beloved horrors, and leaves me to the hateful light?

188.                    *Ohimé, se tanto amate*

If you like so much, alas, to hear me say Alas, why then do you cause to die him who says Alas. If I die you will be able to hear only one languid, sad Alas. But if you wish my heart to have life from you, then you will have from me thousands and thousands of sweet Alas's.

189. *Non schivar, non parar*

They do not wish to dodge, to parry, nor withdraw, as here skill has a part. They do not give blows now feigned, now full, now few. Darkness and madness prevent the practice of the art. You hear the swords; the iron clashes horribly in the midst and the foot does not leave its imprint; the foot is always firm but the hand constantly in motion lowers its blade in vain thrusts; avowedly the shame arouses disdain for the vengeance, and vengeance then renews the shame. Whence always in striking, always in haste, a new stimulus is added, and the more a new wound from time to time is delivered more often is a wound held back; it is no use to wield the sword and blows; they hit each other with the butt ends and, having become wicked and crude, they strike together with helms and with shields.

200. *Verso do primeiro tom*

And my spirit hath rejoiced in God my Saviour.

201a. *Da Jesus an dem Kreuze stund*

As Jesus was standing by the cross
His body so sorely afflicted with bitter pains:
The Seven words that Jesus spoke—
Consider them well within your heart.

201b. *Und um die neunte Stunde*

And about the ninth hour Jesus cried with a loud voice, saying, Eli, Eli, lama sabachthani? that is to say, My God, my God, why hast thou forsaken me? Matthew 27:46

202. *Saul, Saul*

Saul, Saul, why persecutest thou me? . . . it is hard for thee to kick against the pricks. Acts 9:4,5

203. *Io lo vedo*

I see it, ye fair eyes,
That my boldness is more than boldness.
But I cannot fail to follow
Both my star and my stars.
When I turn my thought
To you, dear beloved eyes,
To my lips uncalled
Come the sighs.
Nor can I check,
Either by force or by fraud,
The desires which dwell always in my heart
Together with a flood of fires.

205. *Auf, mein Geist*

Rise, my soul. And praise now
God's kindness and paternal faithfulness.
He it is, who, as long as I live,
Frees me of all care.
Therefore in His honor alone
Shall my music be heard.

206. *Ecco la lettra*

Arsamene: Here is the letter, Elviro.
Elviro: Are you determined . . .
Ars: If I am to remain among the living . . .
Elv: That I shall bear it to Romilda?

Ars: Or else I shall descend among the dead.
Elv: You are not writing anything except that you wish to speak to her?
Ars [or Elv]: I am not going, Sir, I . . .
Elv [or Ars]: I have considered it well.
Elv: Tell me to go with good fortune.
Ars: Thus do I wish it to thee: go.
Elv: Leave it to me. I will serve you truly.
Ars: [For] a loving heart pierced by sorrow over a faithless beauty death remains. It has no other life than hope.
Elv: Sir, I had forgotten: you did not say to me: go with good fortune.
Ars: Go, for my heart repeats it to thee at every moment.
Elv: Say it to me, won't you?
Ars: Go with good fortune.
Elv: Now, leave things to me.

207. *Miserunt ergo sortem*

They therefore cast lots, and lo! the lot fell upon Jonah; therefore the men of the ship said to him:
"Tell us for what cause is this evil. What is thy business? What is thy country? What is thy journey? Or of what people art thou?"
"I am a Hebrew and I fear the Lord God of heaven, who made the sea and the dry land."
"What shall we do to thee so that this tempest shall cease which threatens us with destruction?"
"Take me up and cast me into the sea! . . . and this tempest shall cease. Because I know that for my sake this great tempest is upon you."
The sailors took up Jonah and cast him into the sea: and the sea ceased from its raging. And the Lord prepared a great fish to swallow up Jonah who prayed to his God out of the belly of the great fish and said:
"Thou art just, O Lord, and right is thy judgment, thou art powerful and there is none who can resist thy will. Thou hast cast me forth into the depth of the sea and thy waves have passed over me. Thou art just, O Lord, and right is thy judgment, but when thou shalt be angry, thou shalt remember mercy. Be appeased Lord, forgive, Lord, and have mercy . . . I am cast away out of the sight of thine eyes, thy wrath is kindled and against me the tempest has arisen and the winds have raged and the floods have swelled, the deep has closed me round about and the great fish has swallowed me up. Why hast thou cast forth thy servant forever? Be appeased, O Lord, forgive, Lord, and have mercy."
Based mainly on the Book of Jonah

209. *Poca voglia di far bene*

Small desire to do good. Living in gladness, making merry, keep me fresh and corpulent. Fatigue is no friend of mine; and while I live thus, every day is for me a holiday. Diri, diri, diri, di.

213. *Wende dich, Herr*

Altus: Turn thee, oh Lord, and be merciful unto me. Since I am lonely and wretched, the anguish of my heart is great, lead me out of all my troubles. Behold my misery and wretchedness: and pardon all my sins.

Bassus: Is not Ephraim my dear son and my beloved child? Because I remember well what I have said to him, therefore my heart yields toward him, so I must have mercy on him.

214. *Wachet auf, ruft uns die Stimme*

Awake, thus calls us the voice
Of the guardians high up on the tower:
Awake, awake, thou city of Jerusalem.

Midnight is this hour called
Which summons us with a loud voice:
Where are ye, wise virgins?
Lo, the bridegroom cometh,
Arise, arise, take the lamps, alleluia!
Make ready for the wedding!
You shall go and meet him.

218. *Aleph. Ego vir*

*Aleph.* I am the man that hath seen affliction by the rod of his wrath. *Aleph.* He hath led me, and brought me into darkness, but not into light. *Aleph.* Surely against me is he turned; he turneth his hand against me all the day. *Beth.* My flesh and my skin hath he made old; he hath broken my bones. *Beth.* He hath builded against me, and compassed me with gall and travail. *Beth.* He hath set me in dark places . . . that I cannot get out: he hath made my chain heavy. *Ghimel.* Also when I cry and shout, he shutteth out my prayer. *Ghimel.* He hath inclosed my ways with hewn stone, he hath made my paths crooked.

Jerusalem, Jerusalem, turn thee to the Lord thy God.

Largely from Lamentations 3:1–9

221. *Di bellezza e di valore*

Every honor for beauty and valor, every glory shall be given to you; and may it be echoed everywhere. Long life for Venus and Mars.

222. *Lasciatemi morir*

Let me die, cruel stars,
Because living among enemies is slavery.
If, in heaven above, my fall was decreed,
I can never rise again.
The weapons of love are never to be trusted:
Let me die, cruel stars.

225. *Le Ciel protège les héros*

Heaven protects the heroes.
Go, Admetus, go, Alcides.
The god who presides over the waters
Commands me to calm the waves,
Go, go, pursue the faithless one.
Withdraw, angry winds,
Return within your deep prisons,
And allow the sweetest zephyrs
To reign over the waves.

226. *Dialogue entre Madeleine et Jésus*

"Woe is me, unhappy Magdalen! They have taken away my Lord, whom I loved, who loved me, in whom I lived, who deigned to die for me. And I know not where they have laid him. Woe is . . ."

"Woman, why weepest thou? Why dost thou sigh? Whom seekest thou?"

"Sir, if thou hast taken my Christ hence, tell me where thou hast laid him, and I will take him away."

"Mary!"

"Jesus mine!"

"Do not touch me, for I am not yet ascended to my Father. But go to my brethren and say to them: 'I ascend to my Father and to your God.'"

"Permit me, Lord, to touch your sacred wounds."

"Do not touch me."

"Shall I not kiss thy wounds? . . . Embrace thy feet?"

Based mainly on John 20:15–17

227. *Señor mio Jesu Cristo*

My Lord Jesus Christ, true God and man, being as thou art, and because I love thee above all things, it grieves me with all my heart to have offended thee. Before thy court, oh Judge of the living and the dead, confessing my sins, humbly I present myself.

228. *Adonis Tod*

Where might the beautiful hunter be,
Adonis, my soul?
For whom in loving anguish
I often grieve and languish.
Oh bitter pain,
Beyond which nothing can be:
A wild boar has slain him, ah,
Whom I shall forever lament.
Oh anguish and grief.
Ah, Adonis is dead,
My Adonis is dead.

235. *Liebster Herr Jesu*

Dearest Lord Jesus, where dost thou abide so long?
Come, then, I am so full of dread here on earth.
Come, then, and take me whenever thou wilt
Away from the world's heavy burdens.
It is enough, Lord, so come to deliver my afflicted soul from wickedness;
I am so faint with grieving and sighing,
And so full of wearisome tears.
Come, then, Lord Jesus, come, come, where dost thou abide so long?
Come, then, I am so full of dread here on earth.

241. *Tra cruci funeste*

Amidst fatal tortures may the bitter harshness of cruel death be prepared for the wicked one. Jealous rage in my embittered soul urges my spirit to deprive the wicked traitor of life. Vengeance! Vengeance!

244. *Un balen*

A flash of uncertain hope
Is the only ray which remains to me
Amid the clouds of sorrow.
But my sufferings are real,
And deceptive is the hope
Which shines upon this heart.

254. *Himmel, du weisst meine Plagen*

Heaven, thou knowest my sorrows,
To thee, to thee only are they known.
Thy hand will always inflict wounds;
Should not there be also some remedy
For the grief I must carry in my breast?
Cool the burning pains,
Soothe my anguish.

257. *Cantate Domino*

[Praise ye the Lord.] Sing unto the Lord a new song, and his praise in the congregation of saints.

Let Israel rejoice in him that made him: let the children of Zion be joyful in their King.

Let them praise his name in the dance: let them sing praises unto him with the timbrel and harp.

For the Lord taketh pleasure in his people: he will beautify the meek with salvation.

Let the saints be joyful in glory: let them sing aloud upon their beds.

Let the high praises of God be in their mouth, and a two-edged sword in their hand.

To execute vengeance upon the heathen, and punishments upon the people;

To bind their kings with chains, and their nobles with fetters of iron;

To execute upon them the judgment written: this honour have all his saints. [Praise ye the Lord.]                    Psalm 149

### 258.                    *Mitilde, mio tesor*

Mitilde, my treasure, so swiftly then does wicked fate steal thee from me: alas, how near is the end of any joy to falling into the sorrow of bitter torment. Thou leavest me here alone where I gaze upon a dark region of rough rocks and high cliffs which, breathing terror, fear, and death, threaten ultimate fate to my life.

Thou well knowest the bitter tears that I shed for these eyes, beloved hope of my heart, and thou did'st behold the sparks which, kindling my heart, made me the victim of love.

But with whom, oh Lord, do I speak? Who listens to my laments? For, alas, these loving lips speak in vain to the pitiless breezes, the heedless winds, the trees, the stones, and the unfeeling plants.

Shady groves, ancient trees, you temper my suffering; thus at least my heart can hope for a truce with its sorrows.

### 262.                    *Deh lascia, o core*

Desist, my heart, from seeking relief
For the moment.
And return, then, with greater grief to weeping
Which is my delight.

### 266.                    *Qui dat nivem*

He giveth snow like wool: he scattereth the hoarfrost like ashes.
                              Psalm 147:16

### 267.                    *Fahret wohl*

Farewell, ye beloved eyes,
Red lips, fare ye well.
Let me consume the glances of your eyes
And the roses of your lips,
For I shall leave you.
Thy image dwells within my soul
Which feels only your presence.
I am yours, even in the grave
Where my body will be entombed.

### 272.                    *Chor der Seligen*

Holy is our God, the Lord Sabaoth.
The Lamb which was slain is worthy to receive adoration, praise
     and thanks.                    Based in part on Revelation 5:12

### 273.                    *Fiero acerbo*

Bold, harsh destiny of my soul, I grieve, I languish, I die, for far from my bosom is the darling whom I adore. And to make my sorrow greater, for greater torment, my idol does not yet know that I die for him. With useless blushing, since the ardor which I have in my bosom has forbidden me to speak, it does not even wish me to mark paper with [a written record of] my grief.

### 276.                    *Ramage des oiseaux*

These birds, through their sweet warbling
Embellish our accord;

They declare in their language
The happiness of the world.

Answer their song, roving and faithful voice: Echo, strike the air with your harmonious sounds. Repeat with me: my glory is immortal, I reign over a happy people.

### 281.                    *Ma giunge appunto*

*Father:* But he is even now coming. Seest thou not in his face how his heart struggles? From this inner warfare everything is to be hoped.

*Mother:* Eternal clemency, thou hearest the prayers of a grieving mother, ah! abandon not the guilty son! Assist him, and renew in him courage; bring him back at last to thy gentle love.

*St. Augustine:* Friend, ah! what torments the wretched heart suffers! Ah! holy faith, I know thee, I adore thee. But, oh Lord, what dost thou command of me? Shall I be forced to abandon forever the forbidden, but sweet affections of my heart? Ah! if I could . . .

*Friend:* Friend, thou canst do everything if God assist thee; and in so grave a struggle he will assist thee.

### 282.                    *Godi l'amabile*

Enjoy the dear present moment
Which is the true and only happiness of life;
Free from fear, love thy beloved;
Pursue the enterprise
To which a sweet, gentle,
And tender love invites you.

### 285.                    *Da me non speri*

May she not expect a sou from me if I should see the rascal there. If she has gone away, if she has married, may she not come back to me. I will not come here. A thing done is done. I am not so crazy; I do not wish to give up, I do not want to doubt my daring girl who has gone from me thus. May she not expect a sou from me, no, no, no, if she has gone away . . .

### 286.                    *Le virtuose*

The virtuosos who are famous in fa, mi, re—all have been under me. Plain song, thundering notes, trills, cadenzas, big intervals—all they have been able to learn from me.

### 287.                    *Lo conosco*

*Serpina:* I know by those artful little eyes, thieving and sly, that though you say no, they mean for me yes.

*Uberto:* Young lady, you are wrong, you fly too high; both the eyes and I myself say no to you, and this yes is in your imagination.

*S.* But why? Am I not fair, elegant, and witty? Look up; comeliness, see what sprightliness, what majesty!

*U.* (Ah, she keeps tempting me as hard as she can.)

*S.* (It seems to me he is giving in.) Yes, sir . . .

*U.* Ah, go away.

*S.* Make up your mind.

*U.* Ah, you are crazy.

*S.* My affections are for you and you should marry me.

*U.* Oh, what a complication it is for me.

### 291.                    *Allons danser*

Let's go dance under the elms, take heart young maidens, let's go dance under the elms. Young men, get your pipes. Let us rehearse a thousand songs, and to give joy to our hearts let us dance with our swains, but we must not remain alone: let's go dance . . . In town they make much more noise, but are they as gay in their play? Always happy, always singing, simple pleasure, beauty without deceit, are all their concerts equal to our pipings?

292. *Chiamo il mio ben*

I call upon mine own just like this when day appears, when it is hidden. But vain is my pain. The idol of my heart does not answer.

293. *Diane impitoyable*

Pitiless Diana, in vain do you order this horrid sacrifice. In vain do you promise to be propitious to us, to return to us the winds that were chained up by your command. No, outraged Greece will not be avenged upon the Trojans at that price. I renounce the honors which were destined for me, and though it might cost me my life, my daughter Iphigenia shall not be sacrificed.

298. *In vasto mare infido*

In the vast, faithless sea, in the night so dark, do thou the Pole Star defend us. Heavenly dawn, putting to flight the horrors of the night, do thou in thy kindness attend to both our words and our cries.

299. *Mors et vita*

Death and life have fought in wondrous conflict; after death the leader of life, living, reigns.

300. *Achetez à ma boutique*

*La Fleur:* Buy in my shop, choose according to your taste. I content my customers, buy, I keep everything.

   *Irene:* What do I hear?

*La Fleur:* Gauze of Bologna, good eau de cologne, Lyonese vest, fine doublet of Alençon, English steel, fine stockings from Beaucaire, ribbons from Paris, very fair needles, pins, laces, all the right price. Buy.

301. *Bald die Blonde, bald die Braune*

Now the blonde, now the brunette,
Now the lean one, now the stout one,
Oh, the capricious whims,
Oh, that beautiful butterfly!
To give one's soul and body
To the soft glance of only one,
That I consider fair. But, the Devil take it!
To be constantly changing, that is asking too much.

305. *Schlaflied des Sturmwald*

*Sturmwald (gets ready to sleep):* Now let the fellow come; I shall chase him all right. (*He draws his sword and puts it at his side.*) He'll not forget it. (*He takes off his coat and vest and covers himself with them.*) And even though I sleep, he shall not dare. (*Yawns.*) Uah, uah, I shall get the best of him. Hah, hah . . . just make one move, yes, yes . . . feel it (*always fainter*) come on, hah, hah, come on (*sleeps and snores*).

306. *Et zic et zic*

Refrain: And zic and zic and zic and zoc, and fric and fric and froc. When the oxen go two by two, the ploughing is the better for it.

Couplets: (1) Without a shepherd, if the shepherdess is in a lonely spot, everything is a bore for her: but if Sylvander the shepherd goes near her, all picks up around them.

   (2) What do you say about that my dear? And what do you think of it, my gossip? Nothing can be well done except by twos. The people on this earth, my faith, would not last long, if they did not say to each other:

*Repeat refrain*

# INDEX

Reference is made to item numbers, not pages. Ordinary figures (roman type) refer to the items themselves together with the related article in the Commentary; italic figures refer to the Commentary alone. Titles of compositions are italicized, names of composers in capitals and small capitals.